Grammar Workouts!

Masako Yasumaru
Akiko Watanabe

KINSEIDO

Kinseido Publishing Co., Ltd.
3-21 Kanda Jimbo-cho, Chiyoda-ku,
Tokyo 101-0051, Japan

Copyright© 2019 by Masako Yasumaru
　　　　　　　　 Akiko Watanabe

All rights reserved. No part of this publication may be reproduced, stored in a retrieval system, or transmitted, in any form or by any means, electronic, mechanical, photocopying, recording or otherwise, without the prior permission of the publisher.

First published 2019 by Kinseido Publishing Co., Ltd.

Cover design: Nampoosha Co., Ltd.

はじめに

Grammar Workouts! は、「英語が嫌い」「英語が苦手」という学生の皆さんが、基礎レベルから英文法を学習し直すためのドリル形式のテキストです。「使える英語」をめざしてオーラルコミュニケーションが導入されてから 25 年が経過し、以後はコミュニケーション能力の養成に重点が置かれようになりました。そのおかげで、現在の学生さんには、上手に相槌を打って、恥ずかしがらずにジェスチャーを交えて答える「応答力」はあるのですが、文章で自分のことを説明したり自分の意見を述べたりする「発信力」となると、結局単語を並べるだけになってしまい、昔の学生さんとそれほど差がないように見えます。そこで、あえて英文法の基礎学習に立ち返って、学生さんたちの「発信力」を高めるお手伝いをするのが *Grammar Workouts!* のねらいです。

本書は Workout 1 から 15 までの 15 課で構成され、体系だった文法項目を 1 課ごとに学習していく作りになっています。各 Workout のはじめに文法の解説が付いていますので、基礎の基礎から見直しながら、効果的に文法の知識を構築していくことができるでしょう。

以下に特徴を挙げます。
1. ドリル形式を取り入れているため、似たようなパターンを繰り返し学習することができます。記述問題も豊富に用意しており、解き進めるにつれ、抵抗感なく英文を作れるようになります。
2. 自然な会話や「発信力」の養成につながるよう、平叙文ばかりでなく、「〜じゃないの？」「〜だよね？」など、さまざまな文の形をすべてのワークアウトに取り入れています。
3. 最初の数課は代名詞、be 動詞、一般動詞などの基礎的な文法項目ですが、後ろの課に進むにつれて徐々にレベルが上がるよう設計されています。
4. 文法項目の学習内容は基礎的で平易ですが、TOEIC Bridge®や TOEIC®などの資格試験にもつながるよう、ビジネス英語を意識した表現を多く取り入れています。そのため、内容自体と比較すると語彙レベルが若干高くなっていますが、巻末に単語帳を付けていますので、ぜひ活用してください。

ワークアウトを続けて全課を終える頃には、学生の皆さんの英語嫌いや苦手意識が少しでも薄らいで、英語に興味を持ってくれることを願っています。

最後に、本書の制作にあたって、松本明子氏をはじめとする金星堂の皆さんに大変お世話になりました。この場をお借りして、厚くお礼申し上げます。

2019 年 1 月

安丸雅子
渡邉晶子

Grammar Workouts!

Table of Contents

Workout 1	代名詞・名詞の単複	4
Workout 2	Be 動詞	8
Workout 3	進行形	12
Workout 4	命令文	16
Workout 5	一般動詞 [現在・過去]	20
Workout 6	受動態	24
Workout 7	現在完了	28
Workout 8	助動詞	32
Workout 9	不定詞	36
Workout 10	動名詞	40
Workout 11	分詞	44
Workout 12	接続詞	48
Workout 13	前置詞	52
Workout 14	関係詞	56
Workout 15	重要構文	60
	単語リスト	64

Workout 1 代名詞・名詞の単複

人称代名詞には人称・性・数による区別があり、主格・所有格・目的格の形を持つ。1人称とは話し手（私／私たち）、2人称とは聞き手（あなた／あなたたち）、3人称とはそれ以外の人やものを指す。

 空欄に代名詞を書き入れなさい。

	人称	数	意味	主格 〜は、〜が	所有格 〜の	目的格 〜に、〜を	所有代名詞 〜のもの	再帰代名詞 〜自身
人称代名詞	1人称	単数	私	1.	2.	3.	4.	myself
		複数	私たち	5.	6.	7.	8.	ourselves
	2人称	単数	あなた	9.	10.	11.	12.	yourself
		複数	あなたたち					yourselves
	3人称	単数	彼	13.	14.	15.	16.	himself
			彼女	17.	18.	19.	20.	herself
			それ	21.	22.	23.	なし	itself
		複数	彼ら 彼女たち それら	24.	25.	26.	27.	themselves
指示代名詞	近称	単数	これ	28.				
		複数	これら	29.				
	遠称	単数	あれ	30.				
		複数	あれら	31.				

2 CとDの関係がAとBの関係と同じになるよう、Dに適語を書き入れなさい。

	A	B	C	D
1.	brother	sister	son	_____
2.	art	artist	piano	_____
3.	teach	teacher	study	_____
4.	desk	desks	class	_____
5.	egg	eggs	country	_____
6.	roof	roofs	knife	_____
7.	dish	dishes	foot	_____
8.	one	first	three	_____
9.	second	Monday	fifth	_____
10.	fourth	April	eleventh	_____

3 日本語に合わせて_____に適語を書き入れなさい。

1. 医療の進歩は私の予想をはるかに超えている。
   Progress in medical technology is far beyond _____ expectations.

2. 君を私の取引先に紹介しますよ。
   I'll introduce _____ to my clients.

3. その問題の答えはあなた自身で見つけなさい。
   Find an answer to the problem _____.

4. 私は、それについては彼にちゃんと説明しましたよ。
   I explained it to _____ properly.

5. そこの家具と家電はすべて彼のものです。
   The furniture and appliances there are all _____.

6. 彼女の派手な格好は、うちの服装規定に合わない。
   _____ flashy outfit doesn't fit our dress code.

7. 私たちの方は配送の準備はできています。
   _____ are ready for delivery.

8. おたくの方針はうちのとは違うんです。
   Your policy is different from _____.

9. ラムゼイさんがあなたたちの研修担当者です。
   Ms. Ramsay is _____ training officer.

10. 彼らはクリスマスパーティで楽しんだ。
    They enjoyed _____ at the Christmas party.

4 _____ に最も適当な語を書き入れなさい。

1. Japan has four _____ in a year.
2. May is the _____ month of the year.
3. March comes after _____.
4. Winter is the season between fall and _____.
5. The child of your aunt and uncle is your _____.
6. The daughter of your sister or brother is your _____.
7. _____ is the capital of France.
8. The _____ of Japan is about 120 million.
9. USA has 50 _____ and Japan has 47 _____.
10. There are many old _____ and shrines such as Kinkaku-ji and Heian-jingu in Kyoto.

5 すべての名詞・代名詞を複数形にして、全文を書き換えなさい。

1. You are very efficient.

   _____

2. This is a black ballpoint pen.

   _____

3. That is an eagle egg.

4. He is my best friend.

5. It is his third album.

6. That cat on the bookshelf is mine.

7. There is a Bible in the drawer.

8. This is an affordable condominium.

9. That rehabilitation facility is old.

10. I was a baseball player.

6 日本語を英語の文にしなさい。

1. この本は面白い。
2. これは面白い本です。
3. これらの車は新しい。
4. これらは新車です。
5. あれらの自転車は古い。
6. あれらは古い自転車です。
7. それらは彼の猫でした。
8. これは私の教科書です。
9. あれらは君たちの机です。
10. 彼は会計士でした。

Workout 2 Be 動詞

Be 動詞は「～である」という状態と「～にある、～にいる」という存在を表す。

基本例文 She is 20 years old. 「彼女は 20 歳です。」

①否定文：Be 動詞の後ろに not を入れる。
　She isn't 20 years old. 「彼女は 20 歳ではありません。」

②疑問文：Be 動詞を主語の前に出す。
　Is she 20 years old? 「彼女は 20 歳ですか。」

③否定疑問文：Be 動詞の否定の短縮形を主語の前に出す。
　Isn't she 20 years old? 「彼女は 20 歳ではないのですか。」

④付加疑問文：肯定文の後には否定の疑問形を、否定文の後には肯定の疑問形を付ける。
　She is 20 years old, isn't she? 「彼女は 20 歳ですよね。」
　She isn't 20 years old, is she? 「彼女は 20 歳ではないですよね。」

⑤疑問詞疑問文：〈疑問詞＋Be 動詞＋主語〉の語順にする。
　疑問詞自体が主語になっている場合は、〈疑問詞＋Be 動詞〉の語順にする。
　How old is she? 「彼女は何歳ですか。」
　Who is 20 years old? 「誰が 20 歳なのですか。」

 空欄に Be 動詞を書き入れなさい。

	単数・主格 ～は	Be 動詞 ～です／だ	複数・主格 ～は	Be 動詞 ～です／だ
現在	I「私は」	1.	We「私たちは」	4.
	You「あなたは」	2.	You「あなたたちは」	5.
	He「彼は」 She「彼女は」 It「それは」	3.	They「彼らは」 「彼女たちは」 「それらは」	6.

	単数・主格〜は	Be動詞〜でした/だった	複数・主格〜は	Be動詞〜でした/だった
過去	I「私は」	7.	We「私たちは」	10.
	You「あなたは」	8.	You「あなたたちは」	11.
	He「彼は」 She「彼女は」 It「それは」	9.	They「彼らは」「彼女たちは」「それらは」	12.

2 日本語に合わせて_____に適語を書き入れなさい。

1. アロンソ氏は有名なF1レーサーだ。
   Mr. Alonzo _____ a famous Formula One racing driver.

2. ヴァネッサと娘たちは、その時デパートにいなかった。
   Vanessa and her daughters _____ in the department store then.

3. あなたたちはどこに行くの。
   Where _____ you guys going?

4. 私はすごくお腹が空いています。 _____ starving.

5. フランクとトーマスはここのジムでトレーニング中だ。
   Frank and Thomas _____ working out at this gym.

6. 一部の同僚は今、会議室にいます。
   Some of my colleagues _____ in the meeting room.

7. あなたのいとこたちは高校生ですよね。
   Your cousins _____ high school students, aren't they?

8. クルーズ夫妻は仲が良くないのですか。
   _____ Mr. and Ms. Cruise getting along with each other?

9. 今10時半です。 _____ ten thirty.

10. 彼女のクローゼットの中にはたくさんのドレスがあった。
    There _____ many dresses in her closet.

以下の指示に従って書き換えなさい。

①否定文　　　④付加疑問文　　　　　⑦下線部を問う疑問文
②疑問文　　　⑤否定文の付加疑問文　⑧下線部を問う疑問文
③否定疑問文　⑥下線部を問う疑問文

1. This is a newly released computer.
① ___
② ___
③ ___
④ ___
⑤ ___
⑥ ___

2. Nigel was six feet tall in the seventh grade.
① ___
② ___
③ ___
④ ___
⑤ ___
⑥ ___
⑦ ___
⑧ ___

3. They were in the classroom around noon.
① ___
② ___
③ ___
④ ___
⑤ ___
⑥ ___
⑦ ___
⑧ ___

4. <u>His</u> TV program was <u>really interesting</u>, too.

① _____
② _____
③ _____
④ _____
⑤ _____
⑥ _____
⑦ _____

4 ( ) 内の語を並べ替えて、日本語に合う英文を完成させなさい。ただし、文頭に来る語も小文字で示しています。

1. あのスーパーには様々な食料品があります。
   (in / that / there / are / supermarket / foods / various).
   _____.

2. ここから目的地までの距離はどれくらいですか。
   (from / to / the / is / far / here / destination / it / how)?
   _____?

3. エミリーはその朗報を聞いて、喜んでいなかったのですか。
   (to / the / Emily / news / glad / good / hear / wasn't)?
   _____?

4. 特急列車は満員ですよね。
   The (of / train / passengers, / express / full / is / isn't / it)?
   The _____?

5. ジムは昨日、人材管理セミナーを欠席しました。
   Yesterday Jim (on / from / was / managing / absent / people / a seminar).
   Yesterday Jim _____.

Workout 3 進行形

進行形は〈Be 動詞＋ -ing〉の形で「～している、～していた」の意味になり、進行中の動作や習慣的に行っている動作を表す。

基本例文 He is watching TV now. 「彼は今テレビを見ています。」

①否定文：Be 動詞の後ろに not を入れる。「～していない、～していなかった」
　He isn't watching TV now. 「彼は今テレビを見ていません。」

②疑問文：Be 動詞を主語の前に出す。「～していますか、～していましたか」
　Is he watching TV now? 「彼は今テレビを見ていますか。」

③否定疑問文：Be 動詞の否定の短縮形を主語の前に出す。
　　　　　　「～していないのですか」「～していなかったのですか」
　Isn't he watching TV now? 「彼は今テレビを見ていないのですか。」

④付加疑問文：肯定文の後には、否定の疑問形を付ける。「～ですよね」
　　　　　　否定文の後には、肯定の疑問形を付ける。「～ではないですよね」
　He is watching TV now, isn't he? 「彼は今テレビを見ていますよね。」
　He isn't watching TV now, is he? 「彼は今テレビを見ていませんよね。」

⑤疑問詞疑問文：〈疑問詞＋Be 動詞＋主語〉の語順にする。
　疑問詞自体が主語になっている場合は、〈疑問詞＋Be 動詞〉の語順にする。
　What is he doing now? 「彼は今何をしていますか。」
　Who is watching TV now? 「誰が今テレビを見ているのですか。」

1 動詞を -ing 形に書き換えなさい。

1. listen _____
2. go _____
3. look _____
4. play _____
5. study _____
6. come _____
7. write _____
8. see _____
9. get _____
10. run _____

( ) 内の適語を選びなさい。

1. She (is / was / were) doing her homework now.
2. Bill and I (am / was / were) talking with Mr. Brown then.
3. My mother (isn't / wasn't / weren't) cooking at that time.
4. We (isn't / aren't / didn't) singing songs.
5. (Do / Does / Is) your sister cleaning her room now?

 以下の指示に従って書き換えなさい。

①進行形　　　　　④進行形否定疑問文　　　⑦下線部を問う進行形疑問文
②進行形否定文　　⑤進行形付加疑問文　　　⑧下線部を問う進行形疑問文
③進行形疑問文　　⑥否定進行形付加疑問文　⑨下線部を問う進行形疑問文

1. We practice French for the business trips.
①　
②　
③　
④　
⑤　
⑥　
⑦　
⑧　
⑨　

2. The subway runs at 18 miles an hour to maintain punctuality.
①　
②　
③　
④　
⑤　
⑥　
⑦　
⑧　

Workout 3　進行形

⑨ _____

3. <u>Richard</u> will wait for Amanda <u>in front of the station</u> <u>at ten</u>.
① _____
② _____
③ _____
④ _____
⑤ _____
⑥ _____
⑦ _____
⑧ _____
⑨ _____

4. <u>Nicole</u> will <u>attend a meeting at our head office</u> <u>around three</u>.
① _____
② _____
③ _____
④ _____
⑤ _____
⑥ _____
⑦ _____
⑧ _____
⑨ _____

4 （　）内の指示に従って書き換えなさい。

1. I shopped at a nearby supermarket.（進行形に）
_____

2. Our staff will work at the warehouse around two.（進行形の否定疑問文に）
_____

3. Your marketing department conducts a survey.（進行形の付加疑問文に）
_____

4. Ms. Smith is correcting invoices for her customers.（下線部を問う疑問文に）

5. Brian will be taking a shower around nine.（下線部を問う疑問文に）

5 （　）内の語を並べ替えて、日本語に合う英文を完成させなさい。ただし、文頭に来る語も小文字で示しています。

1. 私たちはその時、うちの本社で合併について交渉を行っていました。
We（our / at / office / a merger / head / negotiating / were）then.
We _____ then.

2. 不景気なのに事業を拡大しているのですか。
（spite / the depression / expanding / of / in / are / you / your business）?
_____?

3. ソニアも昨夜、物理の勉強をしていなかったのですか。
（either / studying / last / physics / Sonia / wasn't / night / ,）?
_____?

4. 今朝、あなたは新聞を読んでいましたよね。
（reading / morning / you / you / were / weren't / a newspaper / this / ,）?
_____?

5. フランクは何時に大阪に出発する予定ですか。
（Osaka / time / is / what / leaving / Frank / for）?
_____?

Workout 4 命令文

命令文は動詞の原形を使って、命令・依頼・禁止・勧誘などを表す。

基本例文　You walk fast.　　Tom is quiet.
　　　　　　Tom is afraid to express his opinion.

①命令文：動詞の原形を使って「～しなさい」の意味になる。
　命令文の付加疑問文：〈動詞の原形, will you [won't you]?〉の形で「～してね」の意味
　　　　　　　　　　になる。
　<u>Walk</u> fast.　「早歩きして。」　　Tom, <u>be</u> quiet.　「トム、静かにして。」
　<u>Walk</u> fast, will you?　「早く歩いてね。」
　Tom, <u>be</u> quiet, will you?　「トム、静かにしてね。」

②依頼命令文：〈Please＋動詞の原形〉の形で「～してください」の意味になる。
　依頼命令文の付加疑問文：〈Please＋動詞の原形, will you [won't you]?〉の形で「～し
　　　　　　　　　　　　てくださいね」の意味になる。
　Please <u>walk</u> fast.　「早く歩いてください。」
　Tom, please <u>be</u> quiet.　「トム、静かにしてください。」
　Please <u>walk</u> fast, will you?　「早く歩いてくださいね。」
　Tom, please <u>be</u> quiet, will you?　「トム、静かにしてくださいね。」

③禁止命令文：〈Don't [Do not]＋動詞の原形〉の形で「～するな」の意味になる。
　Don't <u>walk</u> fast.　「早歩きするな。」
　Tom, don't <u>be</u> afraid to express your opinion.
　「トム、自分の意見を言うのを恐れてはダメよ。」

④禁止・依頼の命令文：〈Please don't＋動詞の原形〉の形で「～しないでください」の意
　　　　　　　　　　味になる。
　Please don't <u>walk</u> fast.　「早歩きしないでください。」
　Tom, please don't <u>be</u> afraid to express your opinion.
　「トム、どうか自分の意見を言うことを恐れないでください。」

⑤勧誘命令文：〈Let's＋動詞の原形〉の形で「～しよう」の意味になる。
　否定の勧誘命令文：〈Let's not＋動詞の原形〉の形で「～するのはやめよう」の意味になる。
　勧誘命令文の付加疑問文：〈Let's＋動詞の原形, shall we?〉の形で「～しましょうよ」
　　　　　　　　　　　　の意味になる。
　Let's <u>walk</u> fast.　「早く歩こう。」　　Tom, let's <u>be</u> quiet.　「トム、静かにしよう。」
　Let's not <u>walk</u> fast.　「早歩きはよそう。」
　Tom, let's not <u>be</u> quiet.　「トム、黙るのはやめよう。」
　Let's <u>walk</u> fast, shall we?　「早く歩こうよ。」
　Tom, let's <u>be</u> quiet, shall we?　「トム、静かにしましょうよ。」

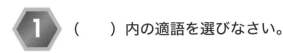 （　）内の適語を選びなさい。

1. (Come / Comes / Coming) here.
2. Koji, (studies / study / studied) English every day.
3. (Is / Are / Be) kind to older people.
4. Don't (run / ran / running) in the classroom.
5. Ms. Green, please (fill / fills / filled) in this form, will you?

 以下の指示に従って書き換えなさい。

①命令文　　　　　　　　⑥禁止・依頼の命令文
②命令文の付加疑問文　　⑦勧誘命令文
③依頼命令文　　　　　　⑧否定の勧誘命令文
④依頼命令文の付加疑問文　⑨勧誘命令文の付加疑問文
⑤禁止命令文

1. You go to school by bicycle.
   ① _____
   ② _____
   ③ _____
   ④ _____
   ⑤ _____
   ⑥ _____
   ⑦ _____
   ⑧ _____
   ⑨ _____

2. You are absent from the annual convention.
   ① _____
   ② _____
   ③ _____
   ④ _____
   ⑤ _____
   ⑥ _____

Workout 4　命令文

① _____
⑧ _____
⑨ _____

3. Ms. Gonzales installs the newly released software.
① _____
② _____
③ _____
④ _____
⑤ _____
⑥ _____
⑦ _____
⑧ _____
⑨ _____

4. George staples those handouts in the meeting room.
① _____
② _____
③ _____
④ _____
⑤ _____
⑥ _____
⑦ _____
⑧ _____
⑨ _____

3 （　）内の指示に従って書き換えなさい。

1. You open spam with an attached file.（禁止命令文に）

_____

2. You register for courses before April 20.（依頼命令文の付加疑問文に）

_____

3. Mr. Lee fills out this application form.（李氏に呼びかける依頼命令文の付加疑問文に）

4. You return our product directly to the factory.（禁止・依頼命令文に）

5. We call a plumber to fix the leaky pipe.（勧誘命令文に）

4 （　）内の語を並べ替えて、日本語に合う英文を完成させなさい。ただし、文頭に来る語も小文字で示しています。

1. ジム、毎年、健康診断を受けなさい。
   (get / year / check-up / every / a medical / Jim,).

2. マイクのことは、しばらくそっとしておいてあげてね。
   (will / for a / alone / leave / while / you / Mike / ,)?

3. 車内では、携帯電話での通話はご遠慮ください。
   (in / on / talk / the bus / don't / your cellphone / please).

4. 誰か、すぐに救急車を呼んでください。
   (immediately / an / call / ambulance / please / someone,).

5. 綾香、当分の間、海外の実務研修に参加するのはやめとこう。
   (the time being / part / not / in / for / take / let's / an overseas internship / Ayaka,).

Workout 5 一般動詞 [現在・過去]

一般動詞は「〜する、〜した」という意味になり、主語が行う動作や状態を表す。主語が I・You 以外の単数で時制が現在の場合は、一般動詞に s [es / ies] を付ける（3人称単数現在形の S）。時制が過去の場合は、主語の人称や単複に関係なく、通常は一般動詞に ed [d] を付ける。

基本例文　　You <u>know</u> her well.　「あなたは彼女をよく知っている。」
　　　　　　　He <u>goes</u> to school by bus.　「彼はバス通学だ。」
　　　　　　　They <u>helped</u> you.　「彼らは君を助けた。」

①否定文：動詞の原形の前に don't / doesn't を付ける。「〜しません」
　　　　　動詞の原形の前に didn't を付ける。「〜しませんでした」

You <u>do**n't**</u> <u>know</u> her well.　「あなたは彼女をよく知らない。」
He <u>does**n't**</u> <u>go</u> to school by bus.　「彼はバス通学ではない。」
They <u>did**n't**</u> <u>help</u> you.　「彼らは君を助けなかった。」

②疑問文：Do / Does を主語の前に付けて、動詞は原形に。「〜しますか」
　　　　　Did を主語の前に付けて、動詞は原形に。「〜しましたか」

<u>Do</u> you <u>know</u> her well?　「彼女をよく知っているのですか。」
<u>Does</u> he <u>go</u> to school by bus?　「彼はバス通学ですか。」
<u>Did</u> they <u>help</u> you?　「彼らは君を助けましたか。」

③否定疑問文：Don't / Doesn't を主語の前に付けて、動詞は原形に。「〜しないのですか」
　　　　　　　Didn't を主語の前に付けて、動詞は原形に。「〜しなかったのですか」

<u>Do**n't**</u> you <u>know</u> her well?　「彼女をよく知らないのですか。」
<u>Does**n't**</u> he <u>go</u> to school by bus?　「彼はバス通学ではないのですか。」
<u>Did**n't**</u> they <u>help</u> you?　「彼らは君を助けなかったのですか。」

④付加疑問文：肯定文の後には、否定の疑問形を付ける。「〜ですよね」
　　　　　　　否定文の後には、肯定の疑問形を付ける。「〜ではないですよね」

You <u>know</u> her well, <u>do**n't**</u> you?　「彼女をよく知っているんでしょ。」
He <u>goes</u> to school by bus, <u>does**n't**</u> he?　「彼はバス通学ですよね。」
They <u>did**n't**</u> <u>help</u> you, <u>did</u> they?　「彼らは君を助けなかったんだよね。」

⑤疑問詞疑問文：〈疑問詞＋do［does / did］＋主語＋一般動詞の原形〉の語順にする。
疑問詞自体が主語になっている場合は〈疑問詞＋一般動詞〉の語順にする。
Why <u>do</u> you <u>know</u> her well?　「なぜ彼女をよく知っているのですか。」
How <u>does</u> he <u>go</u> to school?　「彼はどうやって通学していますか。」
Who <u>helped</u> you?　「誰があなたを手伝ったのですか。」

1 動詞の３人称単数現在形と過去形を書きなさい。

1. talk _____ _____
2. want _____ _____
3. need _____ _____
4. finish _____ _____
5. touch _____ _____

6. live _____ _____
7. use _____ _____
8. stop _____ _____
9. carry _____ _____
10. stay _____ _____

11. break _____ _____
12. buy _____ _____
13. come _____ _____
14. give _____ _____
15. go _____ _____

16. know _____ _____
17. make _____ _____
18. put _____ _____
19. read _____ _____
20. see _____ _____

2 （　）内の適語を選びなさい。

1. My father （get / gets / getting） up at six every morning.
2. Sam （visit / visits / visited） his aunt in the hospital yesterday.
3. （Does / Did / Were） they need my help?
4. Does your colleague （read / reads / reading） a newspaper?
5. I （wasn't / weren't / didn't） work overtime last night.
6. We （don't / doesn't / didn't） watch TV these days.
7. Who （clean / cleans / cleaned） the room every day?
  — Saori （is / does / do）.
8. What time did she （leave / leaves / left） the office?
9. You don't have a driver's license, （do / don't / did） you?
10. Jim, （submit / submits / submitted） a weekly sales report.

以下の指示に従って書き換えなさい。

①否定文　　　④付加疑問文　　　　　⑦<u>下線部</u>を問う疑問文
②疑問文　　　⑤否定文の付加疑問文　⑧<u>下線部</u>を問う疑問文
③否定疑問文　⑥<u>下線部</u>を問う疑問文

1. <u>They</u> usually study <u>for two hours</u> <u>at the library</u>.
① _____
② _____
③ _____
④ _____
⑤ _____
⑥ _____
⑦ _____
⑧ _____

2. <u>The inspectors from Otis Elevator</u> maintain <u>all the elevators</u> <u>in October</u>.
① _____
② _____
③ _____
④ _____
⑤ _____
⑥ _____
⑦ _____
⑧ _____

3. <u>The president's</u> secretary adjusts <u>the schedule</u> <u>once a week</u>.
① _____
② _____
③ _____
④ _____
⑤ _____
⑥ _____
⑦ _____
⑧ _____

4. Gateway Logistics Inc. has twenty-seven branches in Europe.

① _____
② _____
③ _____
④ _____
⑤ _____
⑥ _____
⑦ _____
⑧ _____

4 （　）内の指示に従って書き換えなさい。

1. My children write their diary every night.（否定文に）
_____

2. That patient takes some supplements.（下線部を複数にして疑問文に）
_____

3. That famous actress stays in a gorgeous suite, too.（否定疑問文に）
_____

4. You renewed your license for the antivirus software.（付加疑問文に）
_____

5. Mr. Rodrigo commutes to his office by express train.（下線部を問う疑問文に）
_____

Workout 6 受動態

受動態は〈Be 動詞＋過去分詞＋（by...）〉の形で表され、「（…によって）〜られる、〜される」という意味になる。時制に関係なく、過去分詞は常に過去分詞で、Be 動詞の部分で時制を表現する。

基本例文　Young people love her song.　「若者は彼女の歌が大好きだ。」
→ Her song <u>is loved</u> by young people.　「彼女の歌は若者に愛されている。」
Bob broke the window.　「ボブがその窓を割った。」
→ The window <u>was broken</u> by Bob.　「その窓はボブによって割られた。」

①否定文：Be 動詞の後ろに not を入れる。「〜されない、〜されなかった」
　Her song <u>is**n't** loved</u> by young people.　「彼女の歌は若者に人気がない。」
　The window <u>was**n't** broken</u> by Bob.　「その窓はボブに割られなかった。」

②疑問文：Be 動詞を主語の前に出す。「〜されますか、〜されましたか」
　<u>Is</u> her song <u>loved</u> by young people?　「彼女の歌は若者に人気がありますか。」
　<u>Was</u> the window <u>broken</u> by Bob?　「その窓はボブに割られたのですか。」

③否定疑問文：Be 動詞の否定の短縮形を主語の前に出す。「〜されないのですか、〜されなかったのですか」
　<u>Is**n't**</u> her song <u>loved</u> by young people?　「彼女の歌は若者に人気がないのですか。」
　<u>Was**n't**</u> the window <u>broken</u> by Bob?　「その窓はボブに割られたのではなかったのですか。」

④付加疑問文：肯定文の後には、否定の疑問形を付ける。「〜ですよね」
　　　　　　　否定文の後には、肯定の疑問形を付ける。「〜ではないですよね」
　Her song <u>is loved</u> by young people, is**n't** it?　「彼女の歌は若者に人気なんですよね。」
　The window <u>was**n't** broken</u> by Bob, was it?　「その窓はボブに割られたんじゃないんですよね。」

⑤疑問詞疑問文：〈疑問詞＋Be 動詞＋主語＋過去分詞〉の語順にする。
　　　　　　　　疑問詞自体が主語になっている場合は〈疑問詞＋Be 動詞＋過去分詞〉の語順にする。
　When <u>was</u> the window <u>broken</u>?　「いつその窓は割られたのですか。」
　Whose song <u>is loved</u> by young people?　「誰の歌が若者に人気がありますか。」

⑥ laugh at「〜を笑う」、look after=take care of「〜の世話をする」、run over「〜をひく」、speak to「〜に話しかける」などの群動詞は、まとめて1つの動詞と考える。

The boy <u>was run over</u> by a car.　「その少年は車にひかれた。」

1 動詞の過去形と過去分詞を書きなさい。

1. decide _____ _____
2. move _____ _____
3. admit _____ _____
4. ship _____ _____
5. delay _____ _____

6. destroy _____ _____
7. marry _____ _____
8. supply _____ _____
9. build _____ _____
10. choose _____ _____

11. cut _____ _____
12. find _____ _____
13. give _____ _____
14. hear _____ _____
15. know _____ _____

16. sell _____ _____
17. send _____ _____
18. spend _____ _____
19. teach _____ _____
20. write _____ _____

2 空欄に適語を書き入れなさい。

受動態	前置詞	意味
be covered	1.	〜で覆われている
be disappointed	2.	〜にがっかりしている
be excited	3.	〜に興奮している
be filled	4.	〜でいっぱいである
be interested	5.	〜に興味がある
be married	6.	〜と結婚している
be pleased	7.	8.
be satisfied	9.	10.
be surprised	11.	〜に驚く
be killed	12.	〜に殺害される
	13.	(戦争・事故)〜で死亡する

Workout 6　受動態

be known	14.		〜として知られている
	15.		〜に知られている
be born	16.	[日付・曜日]	〜に生まれる
	17.	[場所・西暦]	
[製品] be made	18.	[場所]	〜製である
	19.	[材料]	[製品] は [材料・原料] から作られる
	20.	[原料]	
[原料] be made	21.	[製品]	[原料] は [製品] に加工される
be made	into		〜化される
be caught	in a shower		22.

 （　）内の適語を選びなさい。

1. These materials for our presentation （am / is / was / were） collected by Walter.
2. The assembly line （am / is / are / were） inspected every Monday.
3. Adams is （watch / watches / watched / watching） a baseball game on TV.
4. Ms. Freestone was （surprise / surprises / surprising / surprised） at the news.
5. Many strange flowers can （see / be see / been seen / be seen） in this country.
6. The pool must （clean / cleans / be cleaning / be cleaned） before July 1.
7. An Asian black bear was （catch / catched / caught / catching） by the hunters.
8. Ellen was （read / reads / readed / reading） by the window.
9. Their term papers will be （finish / finishing / finished / to finish） by next Friday.
10. The station building is made （in / of / from / into） brick.

4 日本語に合わせて_____に適語を書き入れなさい。

1. 『老人と海』はアーネスト・ヘミングウェイによって書かれた。
   The Old Man and the Sea was _____ _____ Ernest Hemingway.

2. 万有引力の法則は、1665年にニュートンによって発見された。
   The law of universal gravitation was _____ _____ Newton in 1665.

3. たくさんの建物がここから見える。
   Many buildings _____ _____ _____ from here.

4. 御社の新製品に大変興味があります。
   I am very _____ _____ your new product.

5. 彼はモスクワ生まれですか。
   Was he _____ _____ Moscow?

5 （　）内の指示に従って書き換えなさい。

1. Many foreigners visit Kyoto.（受動態の文に）

2. Emily took those pictures last Sunday.（受動態の疑問文に）

3. The head coach chose me as a regular, too.（受動態の否定文に）

4. John took his cat to an animal hospital.（受動態の付加疑問文に）

5. They deliver news on the Internet <u>three times a day</u>.（下線部を問う受動態の文に）

Workout 7 現在完了

現在完了は〈have / has＋過去分詞〉の形で表され、「～したところだ、～してしまった、～したことがある」などの意味になる。

基本例文　I <u>have</u> already <u>finished</u> lunch.　「もう昼食を食べ終わった。」
　　　　　　Alice <u>has</u> <u>visited</u> Rome twice.　「アリスは2度ローマを訪れたことがある。」

①否定文：have / has の後ろに not / never を入れる。
　I <u>have</u>n't <u>finished</u> lunch yet.　「まだ昼食を食べ終わってない。」
　Alice <u>has</u> never <u>visited</u> Rome.　「アリスはローマを訪れたことがない。」

②疑問文：have / has を主語の前に出す。
　<u>Have</u> you <u>finished</u> lunch yet?　「もう昼食を食べ終わりましたか。」
　<u>Has</u> Alice <u>visited</u> Rome before?　「アリスは以前にローマを訪れたことがありますか。」

③否定疑問文：haven't / hasn't を主語の前に出す。
　<u>Have</u>n't you <u>finished</u> lunch yet?　「まだ昼食を食べ終わっていないのですか。」
　<u>Has</u>n't Alice ever <u>visited</u> Rome?　「アリスはローマを訪れたことがないのですか。」

④付加疑問文：肯定文の後には、否定の疑問形を付ける。「～ですよね」
　　　　　　　否定文の後には、肯定の疑問形を付ける。「～ではないですよね」
　You've already <u>finished</u> lunch, <u>have</u>n't you?　「もう昼食は食べ終えたんですよね。」
　Alice <u>has</u> never <u>visited</u> Rome, has she?　「アリスはローマを訪れたことがないんですよね。」

⑤疑問詞疑問文：〈疑問詞＋have / has＋主語＋過去分詞〉の語順にする。
　　　　　　　　疑問詞自体が主語になっている場合は〈疑問詞＋have / has＋過去分詞〉の語順にする。
　How many times <u>has</u> Alice <u>visited</u> Rome?　「アリスは何回ローマを訪れたことがありますか。」
　Who <u>has</u> <u>broken</u> the vase?　「誰が花瓶を割ってしまったのですか。」

- have gone (to)　　　結果「～へ行ってしまった」
- have been (to)　　　経験「～へ行ったことがある」、完了「～へ行ってきたところだ」
- have been in　　　　継続「～にずっと居る」

1 動詞の過去形と過去分詞を書きなさい。

1. be _____ _____
2. begin _____ _____
3. bring _____ _____
4. cut _____ _____
5. eat _____ _____
6. get _____ _____
7. leave _____ _____
8. lose _____ _____
9. think _____ _____
10. write _____ _____

2 空欄に日本語訳を書き入れなさい。

結果 完了	just「ちょうど」（過去分詞の前） already「すでに、もう」（過去分詞の前） yet「疑もう、すでに」「否まだ」（過去分詞の前か文末）
He has just left Japan.	彼はちょうど日本を 出発 1._____。
She has already left for Sendai.	彼女はすでに仙台に向けて 出発 2._____。
Have you found a job yet?	あなたはもう仕事を 見つけ 3._____。
My order hasn't arrived yet.	私が注文した品はまだ 到着 4._____。
経験	never「一度も〜ない」（過去分詞の前） ever「疑今までに」（過去分詞の前） once「一回、かつて」（文末）、X times「X回」（文末）、before「以前」（文末）
She has stayed at the Ritz-Carlton many times.	彼女はリッツカールトンに何度も 宿泊 5._____。
We have never climbed Mt. Fuji.	私たちは富士山に一度も 登 6._____ない。
Have you ever seen *Star Wars*?	今までに『スター・ウォーズ』を 観た 7._____。
継続	for「〜の間」、since「〜以来、〜から」
I have known him since we were children.	私は、子供の頃からずっと彼のことを 知 8._____。
They have lived in Osaka for 20 years.	彼らは20年間ずっと大阪に 住 9._____。

Workout 7 現在完了

3 _____ の語句を使い、日本語に合わせて下線部を完成させなさい。

1. 夫はちょうど帰宅したところだ。　`just come`
   My husband _____ home.

2. 私はまだ誰に投票するか決めてない。　`decide`
   I _____ whom to vote for yet.

3. もうクリスマスカードは書いてしまいましたか。　`write`
   Have you _____ Christmas cards yet?

4. マクレーンさんはメガネを失くしてしまった。　`lose`
   Mr. MacLaine _____ his glasses.

5. 彼は何回かそのアプリを使ったことがある。　`use`
   He _____ the application several times.

4 日本語に合わせて_____に適語を書き入れなさい。

1. サッカーの試合はちょうど始まったところだ。
   The soccer game _____ _____ _____.

2. 地下鉄はまだ駅に到着していない。
   The subway _____ _____ at the station _____.

3. 契約書にもう署名しましたか。
   _____ you _____ a contract _____?

4. 今までに何回出張で中国に行ったことがありますか。　—1回だけです。
   How _____ _____ have you been to China on business? —_____ _____.

5. 彼らが結婚して半年になる。
   Six months _____ _____ _____ they got married.

日本語に合わせて_____に適語を書き入れなさい。

1. ①私は15年間ずっと福岡に住んでいる。
   I have _____ in Fukuoka _____ 15 years.

   ②私は2011年からずっと福岡に住んでいる。
   I have _____ in Fukuoka _____ 2011.

   ③福岡に住み始めてどのくらいになりますか。
   _____ _____ _____ you _____ in Fukuoka?

   ④私は以前福岡に住んだことがある。
   I _____ _____ in Fukuoka _____.

   ⑤私は福岡には一度も住んだことがない。
   I _____ _____ _____ in Fukuoka.

   ⑥これまでに福岡に住んだことはありますか。
   _____ you _____ _____ in Fukuoka?

2. ①シンディは8年間ジョンと会っていません。
   Cindy _____ _____ John _____ eight years.

   ②シンディは去年の8月以降ジョンと会っていません。
   Cindy _____ _____ John _____ last August.

   ③シンディはちょうどジョンに会ったところです。
   Cindy _____ _____ _____ John.

   ④シンディはすでにジョンに会いました。
   Cindy _____ _____ _____ John.

   ⑤シンディはまだジョンには会っていません。
   Cindy _____ _____ John _____.

   ⑥シンディはもうジョンには会いましたか。
   _____ Cindy _____ John _____?

Workout 7　現在完了

Workout 8 助動詞

助動詞は平叙文では動詞の前に付いて、動詞に様々な意味を付け加える働きをする。主語の人称や単数・複数や時制に関係なく、助動詞の後ろの動詞は常に原形になる。

基本例文　She <u>can</u> <u>play</u> the guitar.　「彼女はギターが弾ける。」
　　　　　　You <u>should</u> <u>drink</u> a lot of water.　「たくさん水を飲んだ方がいい。」

①否定文：助動詞に直接 not を付ける。
　She <u>can't</u> <u>play</u> the guitar.　「彼女はギターが弾けない。」
　You <u>shouldn't</u> <u>drink</u> the water.　「その水は飲むべきではない。」

②疑問文：助動詞を主語の前に出す。
　<u>Can</u> she <u>play</u> the guitar?　「彼女はギターが弾けますか。」
　<u>Should</u> I <u>drink</u> a lot of water?　「たくさん水を飲むべきですか。」

③否定疑問文：助動詞の否定の短縮形を主語の前に出す。
　<u>Can't</u> she <u>play</u> the guitar?　「彼女はギターが弾けないんですか。」
　<u>Shouldn't</u> I <u>drink</u> a lot of water?　「たくさん水を飲まない方がいいですか。」

④付加疑問文：肯定文の後には、否定の疑問形を付ける。「〜ですよね」
　　　　　　　否定文の後には、肯定の疑問形を付ける。「〜ではないですよね」
　She <u>can</u> <u>play</u> the guitar, <u>can't</u> she?　「彼女はギターが弾けるんですよね。」
　We <u>shouldn't</u> <u>drink</u> the water, <u>should</u> we?　「その水は飲むべきではないんですね。」

⑤疑問詞疑問文：〈疑問詞＋助動詞＋主語＋be動詞の原形か一般動詞の原形〉の語順にする。
　　　　　　　疑問詞自体が主語になっている場合は〈疑問詞＋助動詞＋be動詞の原形か一般動詞の原形〉の語順にする。
　Why <u>shouldn't</u> we <u>drink</u> the water?　「なぜその水は飲まない方がいいんですか。」
　Who <u>can</u> <u>play</u> the guitar?　「誰がギターを弾けますか。」

⑥助動詞は並べて使用できない：後に来る助動詞を言い換える。
　「来週には運転免許が取れるでしょう。」
　　× I <u>will</u> <u>can</u> <u>get</u> a driver's license next week.
　　○ I <u>will</u> <u>be able to</u> <u>get</u> a driver's license next week.

1 空欄に適語を書き入れなさい。

助動詞	例文	意味
will 過去 1._____ 否定 2._____	I will do my best.	私は最善を尽くす 9._____だ。
	It will be fine tomorrow.	明日は晴れる 10._____。
can 過去 3._____ 否定 4._____	He can speak French.	彼はフランス語を話すことが 11._____
	That car can't be cheap.	あの車が安い 12._____。
	You can come in.	入って来 13._____よ。
may 過去 5._____ 否定 6._____	May I borrow this pen?	このペンを借り 14._____ですか。
	John may be tired.	ジョンは疲れている 15._____。
must 過去：なし 否定 7._____	We must study hard.	私たちは一生懸命勉強 16._____。
	Ann must be angry.	アンは怒っている 17._____。
※must not	You must not smoke here.	ここでは喫煙 18._____。
※don't have to ＝don't need to	You don't have to take off your cap.	帽子は脱が 19._____ですよ。
should 過去：なし 否定 8._____	You should apologize to her.	彼女に謝る 20._____だ。
	They should be in Hawaii now.	彼らは今ハワイにいる 21._____だ。

2 日本語に合わせて_____に適語を書き入れなさい。

1. 2、3時間で戻ってくるつもりです。
   I _____ be back in a few hours.

2. 明日になれば、みんながそのニュースを知るだろう。
   All the people _____ know the news tomorrow.

3. 税金の払い戻しを受けることができます。
   We _____ get a refund on our taxes.

4. ついさっき昼食を食べたんだから、今、空腹なはずがないよ。
   You had lunch a little while ago, so you _____ be hungry now.

5. 好きなもの何でも注文していいですよ。
   You _____ order anything you like.

6. これが最後のチャンスになるかもしれない。
   This _____ be the last chance.

7. 彼女はメールで返事をしなければいけませんか。 ―いいえ、その必要はないですよ。
   _____ _____ reply to you by e-mail?
   ― No, she _____ _____ _____ .

8. マルコムはハリケーン・カトリーナのことを覚えているはずです。
   Malcolm _____ remember Hurricane Katrina.

9. 私には、彼の気持ちを変えることはできないでしょう。
   I _____ _____ _____ _____ make him change his mind.

10. 応募者は流暢な中国語を話せなければなりません。
    Applicants _____ _____ _____ _____ speak fluent Chinese.

3 （　）内の指示に従って書き換えなさい。

1. Suzanne must apologize for her subordinate's failure.

   （過去形の付加疑問文に）
   _____

2. You can submit a simple report by the end of this week.
（「～はずだ」の意味を加えて）
_____

3. Bill can't participate in the training workshop.（未来形の否定疑問文に）
_____

4. We should choose <u>Erick</u> as project leader.（下線部を問う疑問文に）
_____

5. Aya's husband will recover from flu <u>in a week or so</u>.（下線部を問う疑問文に）
_____

4　（　）内の語を並べ替えて、日本語に合う英文を完成させなさい。ただし、文頭に来る語も小文字で示しています。

1. このハイブリッド・カーはガソリン1ガロンでどれくらい走りますか。
（of / on / can / one / far / this hybrid car / gas / how / gallon / go）?
_____?

2. 予算配分のことは全然心配しなくていいよ。
You（about budget / to / allocation / don't / all / need / worry at）.
You _____.

3. 彼らは来月には新製品を出荷しなければならないでしょう。
They（will / new / next / ship / to / their / have / month / product）.
They _____.

4. 会計士なら複雑な税金計算でもできなければいけない。
An accountant（complicated / be / make / able / tax calculations / to / must）.
An accountant _____.

5. 今ならまだ、フューチャメディア社との合併を取りやめられるかもしれない。
We（merger / be / call off / with / to / the / able / may still）Future Media Inc.
We _____
Future Media Inc.

Workout 9 不定詞

不定詞は〈to＋動詞の原形〉の形で表され、以下のような意味を持つ。

1 空欄に日本語訳を書き入れなさい。

	例文	意味
名詞的用法	My dream is to become a physician.	私の夢は医者に 1._____ だ。
	She likes to visit temples and shrines.	彼女は寺社を 2._____ が好きだ。
形容詞的用法	We need a color photocopier to print the leaflets.	チラシを 3._____ カラーコピー機が必要だ。
	New recruits have a lot of things to learn.	新入社員は 4._____ ことが多い。
副詞的用法	They temporarily stopped their service to inspect the system.	システムを 5._____、彼らは一時的にサービスを停止した。
	He was glad to receive an acceptance letter.	採用通知を 6._____、彼は喜んだ。
V+O+to do	Our manager told me to order supplies.	部長が私に備品を 7._____ 命じた。
	I asked her to answer the phone.	私は彼女に電話に 8._____ 頼んだ。
疑問詞+to do	We discussed when to start our sales campaign.	我々は販促キャンペーンを 9._____ 話し合った。
	I'll tell you how to operate this machine.	この機器の 10._____ を教えますよ。
その他の重要表現	It is difficult to assemble the bookshelf by yourself.	一人でその本棚を 11._____ は難しい。
	He is too busy to attend the seminar.	彼は非常に多忙なのでその講習会には 12._____。
	She was kind enough to take me to the dormitory.	彼女は親切にも私を寮に 13._____。

2 日本語に合わせて_____に適語を書き入れなさい。

1. ジャクソンは転職することを決意したんじゃないんですか。
   Didn't Jackson decide _____ _____ jobs?

2. バリーには彼を手伝ってくれるたくさんの同僚がいる。
   Barry has many colleagues _____ _____ him.

3. 素晴らしい景色をみる機会に恵まれますよ。
   You can have a chance _____ _____ the splendid scene.

4. シュナイダーさんは給与支払い名簿を調べるために本社を訪れた。(examine)
   Ms. Schneider visited the head office _____ _____ her payroll.

5. 提出前に報告書を見直すことは大切だ。(review)
   It is important _____ _____ a report before handing it in.

3 次の表現を入れるのに、最も適切な位置を選びなさい。

to book a table for five 「5人分のテーブルを予約する」

1. 5人分のテーブルを予約したいのですが。
   ア I イ would like ウ.

2. ケイティは、月に一度のランチミーティングのために5人分のテーブルを予約したがっている。
   ア Katie wants イ for a monthly luncheon meeting ウ.

3. 彼女は秘書に、フランス料理店に5人分のテーブルを予約するよう命じた。
   She told ア her secretary イ in the French restaurant ウ.

4. パトリックは、いつ5人分のテーブルを予約したらいいか尋ねてきた。
   Patrick ア asked me イ when ウ.

5. ランチタイム時に、5人分のテーブルを予約するのは難しい。
   ア During lunch time イ, it is difficult ウ.

Workout 9 不定詞

日本語に合わせて、不定詞の表現を使って英文を完成させなさい。

1. to open a new store
   ①私は新しいお店をオープンすることを決めた。(decide)
   I _____.

   ②新しいお店をオープンできてうれしい。
   I _____.

   ③私の夢は、新しいお店をオープンすることだ。
   My _____.

   ④新しいお店をオープンできる場所を探している。(look for)
   I _____.

2. to buy a luxury car
   ①彼は高級車を買いたがっている。
   He _____.

   ②彼は私に高級車を買わせたがっている。
   He _____.

   ③高級車を買うために、彼は働いている。
   He _____.

   ④彼には高級車を買うための十分なお金はない。
   He _____.

3. to release their new CD
   ①彼らは、新しいCDを発売することに同意している。(agree)
   They have _____.

   ②彼らは新しいCDを発売しようとした。
   They _____.

   ③私は、彼らに新しいCDを発売するよう助言した。(advise)
   I _____.

   ④彼らが新しいCDを発売することは難しい。
   It _____.

5 2つの文がほぼ同じ意味になるよう、＿＿＿に適語を書き入れなさい。

1. It began raining when my daughter got home.
   It began ＿＿＿＿＿ ＿＿＿＿＿ when my daughter got home.

2. I had to do much homework yesterday.
   I had much homework ＿＿＿＿＿ ＿＿＿＿＿ yesterday.

3. We had no food.
   We didn't have ＿＿＿＿＿ ＿＿＿＿＿ ＿＿＿＿＿.

4. Angela wants to be able to swim.
   Angela wants to learn ＿＿＿＿＿ ＿＿＿＿＿ ＿＿＿＿＿.

5. The cupboard was very heavy, so he couldn't move it.
   The cupboard was too heavy ＿＿＿＿＿ him ＿＿＿＿＿ move.

6 ( ) 内の語を並べ替えて、日本語に合う英文を完成させなさい。ただし、文頭に来る語も小文字で示しています。

1. キミーは営業部の新しい職に応募するつもりです。
   Kimmy (to / in / for / position / department / the sales / the new / apply / intends).
   Kimmy ＿＿＿＿＿＿＿＿＿＿＿＿＿＿＿＿＿＿＿＿＿.

2. 私には直ちにやらなければならない仕事がたくさんある。
   I (to / of / do / have / assignments / a lot) right now.
   I ＿＿＿＿＿＿＿＿＿＿＿＿＿＿＿＿＿＿ right now.

3. 質問がございましたら、お気軽にお尋ねください。
   If (have / questions / you / any), (us / hesitate / ask / do / to / not).
   If ＿＿＿＿＿＿＿＿＿＿＿＿＿＿＿＿＿＿＿.

4. ジェイミーに、わが社の新製品のプレゼンをしてほしい。
   I (to / on / our new product / make / want / a presentation / Jamie).
   I ＿＿＿＿＿＿＿＿＿＿＿＿＿＿＿＿＿＿＿.

5. どこでチケットを買えばいいのか教えてください。
   (to / where / me / you / would / buy / tell / a ticket)?
   ＿＿＿＿＿＿＿＿＿＿＿＿＿＿＿＿＿＿＿?

Workout 9 不定詞

Workout 10 動名詞

動名詞は〈動詞の原形＋ing〉の形で表され、「～すること」の意味になる。また、前置詞の後ろに置かれることもある。

1 空欄に日本語訳を書き入れなさい。

	例文	意味
主語になる動名詞	Eating an apple every day is good for your health.	毎日りんごを1個 1._____ は、健康によい。
	Analyzing a monthly report is his job.	月例報告書を 2._____ は、彼の担当です。
補語になる動名詞	His hobby is watching DVDs.	彼の趣味は DVD を 3._____ です。
	My assignment is collecting feedback from customers.	私の仕事は顧客からの意見を 4._____ です。
目的語になる動名詞	I don't like speaking in public.	私は人前で 5._____ が好きではない。
	Enjoy taking part in our leadership training seminar.	リーダー育成セミナーに 6._____ をお楽しみください。
前置詞＋動名詞	My wife is good at making desserts.	妻はデザートを 7._____ が得意です。
	We look forward to meeting you.	あなたに 8._____ を楽しみにしています。

2 日本語に合わせて_____に適語を書き入れなさい。

1. よく眠ることは、精神的ならびに身体的健康に必要不可欠です。
   _____ well is essential for your mental and physical health.

2. 彼のお気に入りの気晴らしはバイクに乗ることです。
   His favorite pastime is _____ motorcycles.

3. ダニエル・パンサーは、最新の小説『森』を出版することを延期した。(publish)
   Daniel Panther put off _____ his latest novel *The Woods*.

4. 私は、定期的に運動することによって、体重を減らすことができた。
   I was able to lose weight _____ _____ regularly.

5. スコットさんが、ニューヨークに着いてからの移動手段を手配することになっている。(arrange)
   Ms. Scott is in charge of _____ transportation for when we arrive in New York.

 次の表現を入れるのに、最も適切な位置を選びなさい。

participating in a day tour　「日帰りツアーに参加すること」

1. 日帰りツアーに参加することが、ここに来た理由です。
   ア Is イ my reason for being here ウ.

2. 価格と効率性の面では、日帰りツアーに参加する方が充実している。
   ア Is more satisfactory イ in terms of price and efficiency ウ.

3. 彼が次の休暇のために提案してきたのは、日帰りツアーに参加することだった。
   ア His suggestion for our next holiday イ was ウ.

4. 彼女がいつか試してみたいのは、日帰りツアーに参加することです。
   ア What she wants to do someday イ is ウ.

5. 残念ながら、ベンは日帰りツアーに参加することを取りやめなければならない。
   Unfortunately, ア Ben イ must cancel ウ.

6. 旅行代理店の社員は、日帰りツアーに参加することを勧めてきた。
   ア The travel agent イ recommended ウ.

7. 私の両親は、試しに日帰りツアーに参加してみた。
   ア My parents イ tried ウ.

8. オリバーは考え抜いた後、日帰りツアーに参加するのを延期した。
   Oliver ア postponed イ after thinking about it over and over ウ.

9. 一緒に日帰りツアーに参加してくれてありがとう。
   Thank ア you イ for ウ with me.

10. 私たちは、日帰りツアーに参加することに興味があります。
    We ア are イ interested in ウ.

2つの文がほぼ同じ意味になるよう、_____ に適語を書き入れなさい。

1. He is a bus driver.
   His job is _____ a bus.

2. It is important for you to learn how to use Excel.
   _____ how to use Excel is important for you.

3. We rode many attractions in the amusement park. We really enjoyed them.
   We really enjoyed _____ many attractions in the amusement park.

4. Betty was drunk and has forgotten slapping Greg in the face.
   Betty was drunk and doesn't _____ slapping Greg in the face.

5. Don't be afraid to make mistakes when you speak English.
   Don't be afraid of _____ mistakes when you speak English.

6. My father is a good cook.
   My father is _____ at cooking.

7. Jeremy loves to collect rare stamps.
   Jeremy is fond _____ _____ rare stamps.

8. Why don't we have a discussion about this over lunch?
   How_____ _____ this over lunch?

9. I accidentally closed a file, but I hadn't saved it.
   I accidentally closed a file _____ _____ it.

10. Make sure to lock the door before you leave the office.
    Make sure to lock the door _____ _____ the office.

 下線部に注意して日本語に訳しなさい。

1. Please remember to post the information regarding the job opening on our website.

2. I don't remember purchasing these books online.

3. I forgot to bring the umbrella with me.

4. Did you forget ordering so much paper for the copier?

5. He stopped to buy a bottle of tea at the vending machine.

6. I can't stop playing games on my smartphone.

6 （　）内の語を並べ替えて、日本語に合う英文を完成させなさい。ただし、文頭に来る語も小文字で示しています。

1. ユニフォームの新しいデザインをすることが最優先事項です。
   (has / a new design / for / top priority / our uniform / creating).

2. 20代の頃富士山に登ったことを今でも覚えている。
   I (in / Mt. Fuji / my twenties / climbing / still remember).
   I _____.

3. 私たちのチームは次のプレゼンの準備を終えた。
   Our team (for / presentation / finished / preparing / the upcoming).
   Our team _____.

4. ネッフル社は、売れ筋のチョコレート菓子の回収を避けたかった。
   Netful (to / best-selling candy-bars / recalling / avoid / wanted / their).
   Netful _____.

5. 私どもの料理教室にご登録くださいましてありがとうございます。
   (signing up for / our / thank / for / cooking class / you).

Workout 10　動名詞

Workout 11 分詞

分詞には〈動詞の原形＋ing〉で「～している」という意味になる現在分詞と、〈動詞の原形＋ed［d］〉で「～される」という意味になる過去分詞がある。

1. 叙述用法：動詞の後に分詞が使われ、補語になる。
    ①〈Be 動詞＋現在分詞〉：進行形「～している」　▶Workout 3

    ②〈Be 動詞＋過去分詞〉：受動態「～れる、～される」　▶Workout 6

    ③〈have / has＋過去分詞〉：現在完了「～したところだ、～してしまった、～したことがある、ずっと～だ」　▶Workout 7

    ④come, go, walk, sit, stand など＋現在分詞：「～しながら…」
        sit, stand＋過去分詞：「～されながら…」
        keep＋現在分詞：「～し続ける」　　　　　など

    ⑤keep, leave＋名詞＋現在分詞［過去分詞］：「A を～のままにしておく」

    ⑥see, look at, hear, listen to, feel など＋名詞＋現在分詞：「A が～しているのを…」
        see, look at, hear, listen to, feel など＋名詞＋過去分詞：「A が～されるのを…」

2. 限定用法：分詞 1 語で名詞を修飾する時は、分詞は名詞の前に置く。
            分詞以外の修飾語と一緒に名詞を修飾する時は、名詞の後ろに置く。
    the stolen money　「盗まれたお金」
    the money stolen from his wallet　「彼の財布から盗まれたお金」

3. 感情を表す分詞形容詞：現在分詞は物の性質を表し、過去分詞は人間の感情を表す。
    The baseball game was exciting.　「野球の試合は白熱するものだった。」
    We were excited at the baseball game.　「私たちは野球の試合に興奮した。」

空欄に日本語訳を書き入れなさい。

	例文	意味
[叙述用法] 補語になる	進行形〈Be 動詞＋現在分詞〉▶Workout 3 She <u>is talking</u> on the phone with her client.	彼女は取引先と電話で 1.＿＿＿＿＿＿＿。
	受動態〈Be 動詞＋過去分詞〉▶Workout 6 A luxury sofa <u>was carried</u> into the president's office.	高級なソファーが社長室に 2.＿＿＿＿＿＿＿。
	完了形〈have＋過去分詞〉▶Workout 7 The bus <u>has</u> already <u>left</u>.	バスはもう 3.＿＿＿＿＿＿＿。
	The audience <u>came running</u> out of the burning cinema.	観客達は火災が発生している映画館から 4.＿＿＿＿＿＿＿出てきた。
	The shop <u>stayed closed</u> all day long.	店は一日中 5.＿＿＿＿＿＿＿ままだった。
	My son <u>left</u> the engine <u>running</u>.	うちの息子は、エンジンを 6.＿＿＿＿＿＿＿にした。
	The shoppers <u>saw</u> a car <u>driving</u> into the store.	買い物客は車が店の中に 7.＿＿＿＿＿＿＿のを目撃した。
	I <u>heard</u> your name <u>called</u> by the receptionist.	私はあなたの名前が受付係に 8.＿＿＿＿＿＿＿のを聞いた。
[限定用法] 名詞を修飾	<u>The smiling boy</u> is my son.	9.＿＿＿＿＿＿＿男の子が私の息子です。
	Do you know <u>the woman sitting next to Max</u>?	マックスの隣に 10.＿＿＿＿＿＿＿女性を知っていますか。
	I found <u>the broken cups</u> around the table.	テーブルの周りで 11.＿＿＿＿＿＿＿カップを見つけた。
	<u>The products launched last month</u> are selling well.	先月 12.＿＿＿＿＿＿＿商品はよく売れている。
感情を表す分詞	The movie *Rocket* was <u>interesting</u>.	映画『ロケット』は 13.＿＿＿＿＿＿＿。
	The baseball stadium was crowded with <u>excited spectators</u>.	野球場は 14.＿＿＿＿＿＿＿観客で満員だった。

Workout 11　分詞

＿＿＿の語句を入れるのに、最も適切な位置を選びなさい。

1. 買い物客たちは、爆発音を聞いてパニックになり、叫びながら走り回った。
   The ア shoppers イ ran around ウ. screaming in panic after the explosion

2. サメやマグロは、生き続けるために泳ぎ続けなければならない。
   ア Sharks and tuna must keep イ to stay alive ウ. swimming

3. ノックスさんは、エアコンから異音がするのを聞いた。
   Ms. Knox heard ア strange sounds イ from the air conditioner ウ. coming

4. カウンターで食事を出している男性を知っていますか。
   Do you know the ア man イ at the counter ウ? serving meals

5. 素晴らしい公演に招待してくれてありがとう。
   Thank you for inviting me ア to this イ performance ウ. amazing

 （　）内の適語を選びなさい。

1. My grandmother lay on the sofa (watch / watches / watched / watching) her favorite TV show.
2. Bobby stood (wait / waits / waiting / waited) for the elevator to arrive.
3. I kept all the windows (closes / was closing / to close / closed) during the typhoon.
4. Maggie felt her cat (to rub / rubs / rubbed / rubbing) up against her leg under the dining table.
5. Six men (work / were working / worked / working) on the bridge were killed in the accident.
6. Subjects (participate / participates / participated / participating) in the clinical trial have to stay in hospital.
7. The watch (makes / was made / made / making) in Switzerland is very expensive.
8. You can see the mountain (cover / to cover / covered / covering) with snow, can't you?
9. The way James talks is really (annoy / annoys / annoyed / annoying).
10. We were (confuses / to confuse / confused / confusing) at the change in her attitude.

4 日本語に合わせて_____に適語を書き入れなさい。

1. 飼育員がウサギに囲まれて座っていた。(surround)
   The zoo keeper sat _____ by rabbits.

2. 上司は新しい規則について説明し続けた。(explain)
   The supervisor kept _____ the new regulations.

3. 支配人は厨房で何かが焦げていることに気づいた。(burn)
   The manager noticed something _____ in the kitchen.

4. 私は木の一番上にいた猫が消防士に助けられるのを見た。(rescue)
   I saw the cat on top of the tree _____ by a firefighter.

5. 昨日の管理職研修セミナーにはがっかりした。
   The management training seminar yesterday was _____.

5 （　）内の語を並べ替えて、日本語に合う英文を完成させなさい。ただし、文頭に来る語も小文字で示しています。

1. 人材派遣を専門に扱っている会社に応募しています。
   I am (temporary staff / specializing in / dispatching / a firm / applying to).
   I am _____.

2. 車両は指定された区画に停めてください。
   You can (designated / park / in / your vehicle / the) lot.
   You can _____ lot.

3. 空港方面へ行く乗客の方は、アンジェラ駅で乗り換えです。
   (change trains / heading for / are required to / the airport / passengers) at Angela Station.
   _____ at Angela Station.

4. 昨日発表された新しい会社規定は、10月1日から施行になります。
   (announced / effective / the new company policy / becomes / yesterday) on October 1.
   _____ on October 1.

5. 子供たちはドキドキする物語に興奮した。
   Children (the / at / thrilling / excited / story / got).
   Children _____.

Workout 11　分詞

Workout 12 接続詞

接続詞は2つ以上の語句や文をつなげる品詞で、主に以下のようなものがある。

1 空欄に適語を書き入れなさい。

	接続詞	意味
時間	1.	～時、いつ～
	2.	～時／～なので、～ように
	3.	～間／が一方～
	4.	～以来／～なので
	until, till	5.
	by the time	6.
	as soon as	7.
条件	8.	もし～なら／～かどうか
	9.	もし～でなければ
	10.	一度～すると
理由	because	11.
	12.	それで、だから
	13.	今や～だから
逆接	14.	～だが、しかし
	15.	～だけれども
その他	16.	そして／そうすれば～
	17.	または／そうしないと～
	18.	～ということ、～だと
	as long as	～する限り［時・条件］
	as far as	～する限り［範囲・程度］
イディオム	both A and B	19.
	＝ not only A but also B	20.
	＝ B as well as A	21.
	not A but B	22.
	either A or B	23.
	neither A nor B	24.

2 （ ）内の適語を選びなさい。

1. They were complaining about their supervisor (if / while) they were having lunch.
2. Giles knew the new regulation well, (so / because) he was put in charge of the project.
3. Applicants need neither previous experience (nor / and) knowledge.
4. Can I stay here (till / when) the rain stops?
5. You cannot go back to the exhibition (and / once) you go through the exit gate.
6. Don't miss the bus, (or / when) you'll have to wait a while for the next one.
7. Let me know (since / when) you finish painting the living room walls.
8. You can discard plastic (as well as / as soon as) paper in the box.
9. I wonder (whether / till) Taylor will appear soon.
10. (Unless / If) you don't register for the conference by tomorrow, you have to pay the regular fee.

3 日本語に合わせて_____に適語を書き入れなさい。

1. アレックスが歯科医院に電話した時、診療時間外だった。
   _____ Alex called the dental clinic, the office was closed.

2. 電車に乗っている間、ほとんどの通勤客はスマートフォンでニュースを読んでいる。
   Most commuters read the news on their smartphone _____ they are riding the train.

3. 写真集を買って以来、私はその写真家の大ファンです。
   I have been a huge fan of the photographer _____ I bought his photo book.

4. 販売営業部にスタッフが足りないので、サンダースさんは異動になった。
   Mr. Sanders was transferred to the sales department _____ they are short of staff.

5. 今はもうその件は解決したから、心配しなくていいよ。
   _____ _____ the issue has been settled, you don't have to worry about it.

6. 飛行機で北海道に行くことになっていたが、機材故障のせいで飛行機が飛ばなかった。
_____ I was supposed to go to Hokkaido by plane, the flight was canceled due to mechanical trouble.

7. 新品が届くまでは、私のノートパソコンを使ってくれませんか。
Would you use my laptop _____ a new one is delivered?

8. スタッフルームの掲示板を確認してください。さもないと、重要な伝達事項を見逃しますよ。
Look at the board in the staff room, _____ you won't get important messages.

9. 私が知る限り、トーマスはアシスタントの募集に応募しなかったですよ。
_____ _____ _____ I know, Thomas didn't apply for the position of assistant.

10. 彼が飲みたかったのは、コーヒーではなくコーラだ。
He wanted to drink _____ coffee _____ cola.

4 の語句を入れるのに、最も適切な位置を選びなさい。ただし文中に来る単語が大文字に、文頭に来る接続詞が小文字になっていることがあります。

1. 彼女はインフルエンザになったので、美容院の予約をキャンセルした。
ア She had the flu, イ she canceled her appointment at the beauty salon.　`since`

2. 私は何度も起こそうとしたが、同僚は眠り続けた。
ア I tried to wake up my colleague many times, イ he kept sleeping.　`though`

3. 会議が終わった途端、彼はトイレに駆け込んだ。
ア He rushed into a bathroom イ the meeting finished.　`as soon as`

4. 住宅ローンの利子が下がらない限り、新築の家を買うことはできない。
ア The mortgage interest drops, イ we cannot purchase a new house.　`unless`

5. ニックはひとたび決心すると、絶対に考えを変えない。
ア Nick never changes his mind イ he decides to do something.　`once`

6. 全商品が午前中に売り切れたので、パン屋は正午に閉店した。
ア The bakery closed at noon イ all the products sold out in the morning.　`because`

7. 私たちが退社するまでに、エレベーターの点検は終わりますか。
   ア Will the elevator inspection be finished イ we leave our office?   by the time

8. バス停まで走りなさい、そうしないと最終バスに間に合いませんよ。
   ア Run to the bus stop, イ you will not be able to catch the last bus.   or

9. 大雨のせいで、列車が遅延するのではないかと心配です。
   ア I'm afraid イ trains will be delayed due to heavy rain.   that

10. ログインするには、メールアドレスかユーザーネームのいずれかをご入力ください。
    ア To log in, enter イ your e-mail address or your user name.   either

5   ＿＿に入れる接続詞を以下より１つ選びなさい。ただし各接続詞は１度しか使えません。文頭に来る場合は、語頭を大文字に直しなさい。

and / as / as soon as / because / either / if / that / though / till / while

1. ＿＿＿＿＿＿ I placed the order online, I found the number of products to be wrong.

2. Julia wants to fly to Chicago today ＿＿＿＿＿＿ she has a meeting tomorrow morning.

3. Board this train, ＿＿＿＿＿＿ you can be in time for your lecture.

4. We failed to close the final contract ＿＿＿＿＿＿ our team prepared well.

5. The company picnic will be canceled ＿＿＿＿＿＿ it rains tomorrow.

6. Do I have to wait in the lobby ＿＿＿＿＿＿ my name is called?

7. ＿＿＿＿＿＿ my father likes traveling, my mother doesn't.

8. ＿＿＿＿＿＿ Sally or I can help you organize the upcoming reception.

9. Now ＿＿＿＿＿＿ he has lived in Spain for five years, Henry must know many popular sightseeing spots there.

10. ＿＿＿＿＿＿ almost everyone expected, Dow Jones Average is rising.

Workout 13 前置詞

前置詞は名詞・代名詞・動名詞の前に置く語で、日本語の「の、を、に、へ」などの助詞に近い働きをする。

 空欄に前置詞を書き入れなさい。

前置詞	意味
at	場所・時の一点、時刻、速度「〜に」「〜で」
1.	場所・時の内部「〜の中に」、月・季節・年「〜に」、着用「〜を着て」、経過「〜経てば、〜後に」
2.	接触「〜の上に」、日付や曜日「〜に」、主題「〜について」
3.	方向・運動「〜を横切って」「〜に渡って」
4.	方向・運動「〜に沿って」
5.	周囲「〜の周りに」「〜を取り巻いて」
6.	貫通「〜を通って、貫いて」、仲介「〜を通じて」、期間「〜中」
7.	出発点・原料「〜から」、出身「〜出身で」
to	方向・到達点「〜へ」「〜に向かって」
8.	方向「〜へ」、期間「〜の間（数字や a(n) と一緒に使って、継続する期間の長さを表す）」、目的・原因「〜のため」、対象「〜に対して」、観点「〜にとって」
during	期間「〜の間（the や代名詞の所有格と一緒に使って、特定の期間を表す）」
between	期間・場所「〜の間に」「〜の中間に」
among	位置・対象「〜の間に（で）」、部分「〜の中の1つ［1人］」
of	所属「〜の」、材料・分離「〜から」、関連「〜について」
near	近接「〜の近くに」
9.	近接「〜のそばに」、手段「〜によって」、期限「〜までに」
until, till	継続「〜までずっと」
10.	同伴「〜と一緒に」、関連「〜に関して」、道具「〜を使って」
11.	不所持「〜なしで」「〜しないで」
12.	時間・順序の前「〜の前」

13.	時間・順序の後「〜の後」
in front of	場所の前「〜の前に、〜の正面に」
14.	場所の後「〜の後ろに、〜の裏に」「〜に遅れて」
15.	方向「〜の中へ」
out of	方向「〜の外へ」、対象「〜のうち」
over	垂直的に真上「〜の上に」「〜を越えて」、超過「〜以上」、従事「〜しながら」
16.	垂直的に真下「〜の下に」、下位「〜未満で」
above, beyond	漠然と上方「〜より上に」「〜よりも高い所に」、超越「〜を越えて」
below	漠然と下方「〜より下に」「〜よりも低い所に」、不足「〜より劣って」

2 （　）内の適語を選びなさい。

1. The retirement party starts （at / in / on） five o'clock.
2. I am taking the writing course （at / in / on） Tuesdays.
3. Our boss will be out of the office （at / in / on） the morning, won't he?
4. Mr. Usher is from Victoria （at / in / on） Canada.
5. Can I put up a poster for our new product （at / in / on） the wall?
6. Let's meet （at / in / on） the bus stop after the class.
7. I'll be there （at / in / on） 30 minutes.
8. We have no time to take a rest （at / in / on） Monday morning.
9. Doesn't the class have a final exam （at / in / on） the end of the term?
10. When is the lecture （at / in / on） lifestyle diseases?

3 日本語に合わせて＿＿＿に適語を書き入れなさい。

1. 新しくオープンした美容室は、その通りを渡ったところにあります。
   The new hair salon is ＿＿＿＿＿＿＿＿ the street.

2. 幼稚園児が川に沿って歩いている。
   The kindergarten children are walking ＿＿＿＿＿＿＿＿ the river.

3. この辺りに大きな公立図書館はありますか。
   Is there a big public library ＿＿＿＿＿＿＿＿ here?

4. テムズ川はロンドンを通って流れている。
   The River Thames flows _____ London.

5. 福岡支店の新しい部長は北海道出身です。
   The new manager of the Fukuoka branch office is _____ Hokkaido.

6. この電車はヒースロー空港行きですか。
   Is this train bound _____ Heathrow Airport?

7. 全応募者の中でエミリー・ハニガンが編集主任に最も適しているだろう。
   Emily Hannigan will be the best senior editor _____ all the candidates.

8. 寂しくなると、私は家族の写真を見ます。
   When I feel lonely, I look at the picture _____ my family.

9. 車のない、田舎での生活は想像できない。
   I can't imagine life in the countryside _____ a car.

10. 夫は、私の頭上の棚に手荷物を置いた。
    My husband put my baggage on the rack _____ my seat.

4   _____ に入れる前置詞を以下より1つ選びなさい。同じ語を2度使ってもかまいません。

behind / by / for / in / on / under / until / with

1. Put these shirts _____ the shelf, will you?
2. My brother has been absent from school _____ a week.
3. Shall we start the quality control meeting _____ five minutes?
4. Many foreigners living in Japan eat their meals _____ chopsticks.
5. We discussed coping with complaints _____ five o'clock.
6. Maria is standing _____ the sink in the pantry, talking with her colleague.
7. The release of the new book is far _____ schedule.

8. Children _____ the age of six can't participate in this event without a parent.
9. Tomatina Festival takes place on the last Wednesday _____ August.
10. Please transfer the money to our account _____ tomorrow.

5 2つの文がほぼ同じ意味になるよう、_____に適語を書き入れなさい。

1. The secretary got on the elevator after the vice president.
   The vice president got on the elevator _____ the secretary.

2. Rachel started learning calligraphy 10 years ago.
   Rachel has been learning calligraphy _____ 10 years.

3. The flight between Tokyo and Amsterdam takes about 12 hours.
   The flight _____ Tokyo _____ Amsterdam takes about 12 hours.

4. Sharon entered the bank to withdraw some money.
   Sharon went _____ the bank to withdraw some money.

5. I had a terrible headache while watching the movie.
   I had a terrible headache _____ the movie.

6. The stylish café near the station is open all year round.
   The stylish café near the station is open all _____ the year.

7. My neighbor has two brown rabbits.
   My neighbor has two rabbits _____ brown fur.

8. Mark was seated in front of me.
   I was seated _____ Mark.

9. We made travel plans for our holidays while drinking coffee.
   We made travel plans for our holidays _____ coffee.

10. Conrad didn't open the envelope before throwing it into the trash can.
    Conrad threw the envelope into the trash can _____ opening it.

Workout 14 関係詞

関係詞は、後ろから直前にある名詞を修飾するのに使われる「のり」のような語である。一言では表現できない長い説明文を付け加える働きをするだけで、訳されることはない。説明される直前の名詞（先行詞）に応じて、使う関係詞は以下の表のように異なる。

説明される名詞	主格	後ろの形	所有格	後ろの形	目的格[省略可]	後ろの形
人	who	・動詞 ・助動詞	whose	・無冠詞の名詞	who(m)	・冠詞付きの名詞 ・代名詞 ・固有名詞
動物や物	which		whose		which	
人、動物や物	that		—		that	
場所	where	・冠詞付きの名詞 ・代名詞 ・固有名詞				
時	when					
理由	why					

  the woman [**who** is running in the park] 「公園でランニングしている女性」
  a building [**whose** rooftop has a heliport] 「屋上にヘリポートがある建物」

that が好まれる場合：前の名詞に the 最上級、the 序数（first, second, last など）、the only「唯一の」、the very「まさにその」が付いている場合、前の名詞が人と（動）物のセットになっている場合

  the highest mountain [**that** I have ever climbed] 「私が今まで登った中で一番高い山」

前に修飾する名詞を持たない what：「～こと、～もの」「今の、昔の～」を表す、よく使われる関係代名詞である。

  what Emily said to her husband 「エミリーが夫に言ったこと」
  what Japan used to be 50 years ago 「50年前の日本」

 （　）内の適語を選びなさい。

1. Judging from his accent, the man (who / which) is talking to our supervisor must be an Australian.

2. We can't repair the old model product (which / whose) components are hard to procure.
3. The presentation class (which / whose) Yoshiki recommended to me was full.
4. Kelly hasn't read the first essay (whose / that) her favorite actor wrote, has she?
5. April is the month (when / where) many new recruits start work in Japan.

2 日本語に合わせて_____に適語を書き入れなさい。

1. チャンさんは、留学中にアパートをシェアしていた友人に会いに、イタリアに行った。
   Mr. Chung went to Italy to see the friend _____ shared a flat with him when he studied abroad.

2. パッケージを一新されたチョコレートバーは売り上げが好調だ。
   The candy bars _____ packages have been redesigned are selling well.

3. テレビ局がネットで配信しているドラマを観るのが好きです。
   I like watching some dramas _____ TV stations are offering online.

4. 以前、販売営業部が利用していたケータリング会社を紹介してくれませんか。
   Would you introduce the catering company _____ the Sales Department used before?

5. バッグの中身が見えるように、バッグを開けてください。
   Please open your bag so that I can see _____ you have in it.

3 _____の語句を入れるのに、最も適切な位置を選びなさい。

1. エレンは、5月30日締め切りの報告書を仕上げたのですか。
   Has Ellen ア completed イ the report ウ ?   whose deadline is May 30

2. 私は毎朝、犬を散歩させている若い女性を見かけます。
   I see ア a young girl イ every morning ウ .   who walks her dog

Workout 14　関係詞

3. 予約を取り消した理由を教えていただけませんか。
Would you ア tell me イ the reason ウ? why you canceled that appointment

4. 春は引っ越し業者が忙しい季節です。
ア Spring イ is the season ウ. when the movers are busy

5. サラは、私が今一番会いたくない人です。
ア Sarah イ is the last person ウ. that I want to see now

4 下線部に注意して日本語に訳しなさい。

1. It turned out that <u>the woman whom I met at the party</u> works in our R&D department.

2. Do you know <u>a hotel which permits guests to stay with their pets</u>?

3. Don't stare at <u>the woman who is standing in front of the store</u>. She is a police officer.

4. <u>The man whose brother is a gold medalist in the marathon</u> was appointed as a coach of our team.

5. I can't forget <u>the day when I received the award</u>.

5 ２つの文がほぼ同じ意味になるよう、＿＿＿に適語を書き入れなさい。

1. Don't you remember the professor? He taught us European Culture at university.
Don't you remember the professor ＿＿＿＿＿＿＿＿ taught us European Culture at university?

2. The young woman has many qualifications. We decided to employ her.
   The young woman _____ we decided to employ has many qualifications.

3. The closing ceremony took place in the conference hall. Mr. Leonard had delivered a keynote speech about ecosystems there before.
   The closing ceremony took place in the conference hall _____ Mr. Leonard had delivered a keynote speech about ecosystems before.

4. His words and actions at the party turned off their guests.
   _____ he _____ and _____ at the party turned off their guests.

5. My guests from Canada visited the temple that has a very picturesque garden.
   My guests from Canada visited the temple _____ garden was very picturesque.

6. The large screen display is very light and thin. They installed it in the domed stadium.
   The large screen display _____ they installed in the domed stadium is very light and thin.

7. The municipal bus is the only public transportation. It takes visitors to Penguin Aquarium.
   The municipal bus is the only public transportation _____ takes visitors to Penguin Aquarium.

8. Our team hasn't decided the schedule of the promotion campaign. When will we start it?
   Our team hasn't decided the day _____ we will start the promotion campaign.

9. Why did he fail the job interview? I'm afraid to ask him the reason.
   I'm afraid to ask him the reason _____ he failed the job interview.

10. I have never met _____ a competent attorney as Mr. Baker.
    Mr. Baker is the most competent attorney _____ I have ever met.

Workout 15 重要構文

① It で始まる文

非人称主語の it や形式主語の it は「それ」とは訳に出さないで、it が指している所から訳し始める。

It is said that our president is going to resign this March.
「わが社の社長は今年の 3 月に辞任するつもりだと言われている。」

It seems that the laundry is temporarily closed for renovations.
「そのクリーニング店は改装のため現在は閉店しているようだ。」

It generally takes at least twenty years to be promoted to manager.
「一般的に、部長に昇進するのは最低でも 20 年かかる。」

It is necessary to pay a deposit of twenty thousand dollars on this condo.
「この分譲マンションには 2 万ドルの頭金を払う必要があります。」

It never occurred to her that she would be transferred to the head office.
「彼女は自分が本社転勤になるとは全く思いもよらなかった。」

It is uncertain whether he is for or against this plan.
「彼がこの計画に賛成なのか反対なのかどうかは不明だ。」

② 第 5 文型

make, get「～を…にする」
keep「～を…にしておく」　　　　leave「～を…のままにしておく」
call「～を…と呼ぶ」　　　　　　name「～を…と名付ける」「～を…に指名する」
appoint, choose, elect「～を…に選ぶ」
think「～を…だと考える」　　　 believe「～を…と思う」
consider「～を…とみなす」　　　find「～が…だと分かる」

He **kept** his divorce a secret for a while.
「彼はしばらくの間、離婚を秘密にしていた。」

We **elected** Ms. Bates chairperson of our committee.
「私たちは、ベイツさんを委員会の議長に選んだ。」

My boss **considers** some of his subordinates careless and incompetent.
「私の上司は、数名の部下を不注意で無能だとみなしている。」

1　日本語に合わせて_____に適語を書き入れなさい。

1. 彼女は無罪であったと、一般的に信じられています。
　　_____ is generally believed _____ she was innocent.

2. ホワイト氏は私の言ったことを誤解したようだ。
　_____ seems _____ Mr. White misunderstood what I said.

3. 祖母が病気から回復するには最低でも3週間はかかるだろう。
　_____ will take at least three weeks for my grandmother _____ recover from the illness.

4. 春にこの川で泳ぐのは危険です。
　_____ is dangerous _____ swim in this river in spring.

5. 彼らがそんな無茶な要求を突っぱねるのも当然だ。
　_____ is only natural _____ they reject such an unreasonable request.

6. あなたがどの大学を出ているかは大して重要ではない。
　_____ doesn't really matter what university you graduated from.

7. 部下たちは、陰では社長のことを「皇帝ネロ」と呼んでいる。
　His subordinates _____ the president "Emperor Nero" behind his back.

8. 高齢者たちは、その電気マッサージ器は使いづらいことに気づいた。
　Senior citizens _____ the electric massager difficult to use.

9. 彼は、犬を公園の木につないだままにしているのを忘れていた。
　He forgot that he _____ his dog chained up to a tree in the park.

10. うちの息子はホラー映画のパンフレットを見ただけで怖がった。
　The mere sight of the brochure of a horror film _____ my son scared.

2　(　)内の適語を選びなさい。

1. It seems (to / that / which) CareerStars.com provides résumé-writing services.
2. Is it possible (to / that / why) get a cash refund without any receipt?
3. As the navigation system is voice-activated, it is unnecessary (to / that / what) operate your touchscreen.
4. It is impossible (to / that / for) our hotel to accommodate a tour of over 20 people on May 3rd because it's fully booked during the Golden Week holidays.

5. It will be convenient (to / that / for) me to meet up near the station since I'm going to take the train tomorrow.

6. It's a mystery (to / for / how) she made contact with our competitor.

7. They (called / telephone / named) Michelle vice chairperson of the town council on Friday.

8. A mathematician who discovered the planet (made / left / named) it Neptune after the god of the sea in Roman mythology.

9. Conrad was arrested on suspicion of robbery and murder, but his parents (believe / regard / wonder) him innocent.

10. If you don't want your baby boy to catch a cold, (consider / appoint / keep) his room warm.

 日本語に訳しなさい。

1. It is said that people who drink too much alcohol have a higher rate of dementia.

2. It seems that Mr. Leonhart is in bad physical condition from stress at work.

3. It has become clear that management decided to sell off our unprofitable department.

4. Many parents think the popular TV program harmful to their children.

5. The President appointed Ms. Freeland Secretary of State in January.

2つの文がほぼ同じ意味になるよう、_____ に適語を書き入れなさい。

1. My father's operation is likely to be a success.
   _____ is likely _____ my father's operation will be a success.

2. Jeremy couldn't master the spreadsheet software easily.
　_____ was difficult for Jeremy _____ _____ the spreadsheet software.

3. You have to visit your clients in person.
　_____ is necessary _____ _____ your clients in person.

4. Deborah was unable to sleep all night because of her terrible toothache.
　The terrible toothache _____ Deborah awake all night.

5. We voted for Ms. Wilkinson and she became a city councilwoman in 2017.
　We _____ Ms. Wilkinson city councilwoman in 2017.

5　（　）内の語を並べ替えて、日本語に合う英文を完成させなさい。ただし、文頭に来る語も小文字で示しています。

1. 部下が新契約の交渉に失敗したのは残念だ。
　It（that / a new / a pity / my subordinate / failed in / is / negotiating）contract.
　It _____ contract.

2. 定期的にバックアップ・ファイルを作成することを強くお勧めします。
　It（that / you / backup files / recommended / regularly create / is strongly）.
　It _____ .

3. 9月末までに納品して頂くのは可能でしょうか。
　Would（it / by / of / to / your products / the end / deliver / be possible）September?
　Would _____ September?

4. 燃料を補給する際に、車のエンジンをかけたままにしないでください。
　(while / your / you / please / car's engine / don't / running / refueling / leave / are).
　_____ .

5. 彼らは、娘が生まれた都市にちなんで彼女をフローレンスと名付けた。
　(after / their daughter / they / the city / Florence / named) where she was born.
　_____ where she was born.

単語リスト

A

a little while ago	成句	つい先ほど
accent	名	訛り、口調
acceptance letter	名	採用通知
accidentally	副	うっかり
accommodate	動	収容する、宿泊させる
account	名	口座
accountant	名	会計士
actor	名	俳優
actress	名	女優
adjust	動	調整する
admit	動	認める
affordable	形	手ごろな
afraid	形	恐れて
against	前	〜に反対して
agent	名	代理人
all year round	副	一年中
allocation	名	分配、割り当て
ambulance	名	救急車
amusement park	名	遊園地
analyze	動	分析する
annoy	動	イライラさせる
annual convention	名	年次総会
antivirus	形	ウィルス対策の
apologize	動	謝罪する
appear	動	現れる、姿を現す
appliance	名	電化製品
applicant	名	応募者
application	名	アプリ
application form	名	申込用紙
apply for / to	成句	〜に応募する、〜に申し込む
appoint	動	任命する
appointment	名	予約
arrange	動	手配する
arrest	動	逮捕する
article	名	記事
assemble	動	組み立てる
assembly line	名	組み立てライン
assignment	名	業務
attach	動	添付する
attend	動	出席する
attendee	名	出席者、参加者
attitude	名	態度
attorney	名	弁護士
attraction	名	呼び物、アトラクション
audience	名	観客
avoid	動	避ける
awake	形	目が覚めて
award	名	賞

B

baggage	名	荷物
bakery	名	パン屋
ballpoint pen	名	ボールペン
be absent from	成句	〜を欠席して
be fond of	成句	〜が好きで
be short of	成句	〜が不足していて
be supposed to do	成句	〜することになっている
beauty salon	名	美容室
best-selling	形	最もよく売れている
board	動	乗る
	名	掲示板
book	動	予約する
bookshelf	名	本棚
bound for	形	〜行きの
branch（office）	名	支社、支店
brick	名	レンガ
brochure	名	パンフレット
budget	名	予算

burn	動	燃える
business	名	事業
business trip	名	出張
by oneself	成句	一人で

C

calculation	名	計算
call off = cancel	成句	中止する
calligraphy	名	書道、習字
candidate	名	応募者
candy-bar	名	チョコレートバー
capital	名	首都
careless	形	不注意な
cash	名	現金
catch a bus	句	バスに間に合う
catch a cold	句	風邪をひく
catering	名	ケータリング、仕出し
chairperson	名	議長
cinema	名	映画
citizen	名	市民
client	名	顧客、取引先
clinical trial	名	治験
closing ceremony	名	閉会式
colleague	名	同僚
collect	動	集める
committee	名	委員会
commute	動	通勤する、通学する
commuter	名	通勤者、通学者
competent	形	有能な
competitor	名	競合他社、ライバル企業
complain	動	不満を言う
complaint	名	不満
complete	動	完成させる
complicated	形	複雑な
component	名	部品
condominium	名	分譲マンション
conduct a survey	句	アンケート調査を行う
conference	名	会議
conference hall	名	会議場
confuse	動	混乱させる
contract	名	契約（書）
convenient	形	都合がいい、便利な
cook	名	料理人
cope with	成句	〜に対処する、〜を処理する
copier	名	コピー機
correct	動	訂正する
create	動	造り出す
cupboard	名	食器棚
customer	名	顧客、客

D

dangerous	形	危険な
deadline	名	締め切り
delay	動	遅らせる
deliver	動	配達する
deliver a speech	句	スピーチをする
delivery	名	配達
dementia	名	認知症
dental clinic	名	歯科医院
department store	名	デパート
deposit	名	頭金
depression	名	不景気
designate	動	指定する
destination	名	目的地
destroy	動	破壊する
directly	副	直接に
discard	動	捨てる、廃棄する
discover	動	発見する
discuss	動	話し合う
discussion	名	話し合い
dispatch	動	派遣する
divorce	動	離婚する
dormitory	名	寮
Dow Jones Average	名	ダウ平均株価
drawer	名	引き出し
dress code	名	服装規定

driver's license	名 運転免許	flight	名 航空便
drop	動 下がる	flu	名 インフルエンザ
due to	前 ～のため、～のせいで	fluent	形 流暢な
		for	前 ～に賛成して
		for a while	成句 しばらくの間
		for the time being	成句 当分の間、さしあたり

E

ecosystem	名 生態系
effective	形 効力を発する、実施される
efficiency	名 効率性
efficient	形 有能な
employ	動 雇う
envelop	名 封筒
essential	形 必要不可欠な
examine	動 調べる
exhibition	名 展示会、展覧会
exit	名 出口
expand	動 拡大する
expectation	名 予想、期待
explain	動 説明する
explosion	名 爆発
express	動 表現する
express train	名 特急列車

foreigner	名 外国人
form	名 用紙
fully	副 十分に
fur	名 毛皮
furniture	名 家具

G

gallon	名 ガロン（約 3.8 リットル）
generally	副 一般に、概して
get along with	成句 ～と仲が良い、～とうまくやる
get married	句 結婚する
glasses	名 メガネ
gorgeous	形 豪華な
grade	名 学年
graduate from	成句 ～を卒業する
gravity	名 引力

F

facility	名 施設
factory	名 工場
fail	動 失敗する
failure	名 失敗
favorite	形 お気に入りの
feedback	名 反応、意見、評価
fill in / out	成句 記入する
final exam	名 期末試験
firefighter	名 消防士
firm	名 会社
fit	動 適合する
fix	動 修理する
flashy	形 派手な
flat	名 アパート

H

hair salon	名 美容院
hand in	動 提出する
handout	名 配布資料、印刷物
harmful	形 有害な
head for	成句 ～に向かう
head office	名 本社、本店
headache	名 頭痛
heavy	形 重い
hesitate to *do*	動 ～するのをためらう

I

illness	名 病気

英語	品詞	意味
immediately	副	ただちに
in charge of	成句	～を担当して
in person	副	直接、じかに
in public	副	人前で
in spite of	前	～にもかかわらず
in terms of	前	～の面で、～の点で
in time	形	間に合って
incompetent	形	無能な
informative	形	参考になる、有益な
innocent	形	無実の、無罪の
inspect	動	点検する、検査する
inspection	名	点検、検査
inspector	名	検査官、検査員
install	動	設置する、インストールする
intend to *do*	動	～するつもりだ
interest	名	利息、利子
internship	名	実務研修、インターンシップ
introduce	動	紹介する
invoice	名	送り状
issue	名	問題

J

job interview	名	就職面接

K

keeper	名	管理人、飼育係
keynote speech	名	基調講演
kindergarten	名	幼稚園
knowledge	名	知識

L

laptop	名	ノートパソコン
latest	形	最新の
launch	動	発売する
laundry	名	クリーニング店
leadership	名	リーダーシップ
leaflet	名	チラシ
leaky	形	水漏れがある
lecture	名	講義、講演
lie	動	横たわる
lifestyle disease	名	生活習慣病
light	形	軽い
lock	動	鍵をかける
log in	成句	ログインする
lonely	形	一人ぼっちの
look forward to	成句	～を楽しみに待つ
lot	名	区画、駐車場
luncheon	名	昼食
luxury	形	豪華な

M

maintain	動	維持する、メンテナンスを行う
make sure	句	確実に～する
manage	動	管理する
management	名	管理、経営者
manager	名	部長
marketing department	名	マーケティング部門
material	名	資料
mathematician	名	数学者
meal	名	食事
mechanical	形	機械の
medical check-up	名	健康診断
meet up	成句	待ち合わせる
mental	形	精神上の
mere	形	ほんの、たったの
merger	名	合併
mile	名	マイル（約1.6キロメートル）
million	名	100万
miss	動	乗り損なう
monthly	形	毎月の、月1回の
mortgage	名	住宅ローン
motorcycle	名	オートバイ
mover	名	引っ越し業者

municipal	形	地方自治体の
murder	名	殺人
mystery	名	不思議、謎
mythology	名	神話

N

navigation system	名	走行指示システム、ナビシステム
nearby	形	近くの
negotiate	動	交渉する
neighbor	名	近所の人
newly	副	新しく
niece	名	姪
number	名	数

O

occur	動	起こる
on business	副	商用で、仕事目的で
online	副	オンラインで
operate	動	操作する
operation	名	手術
opinion	名	意見
order	名	注文品
organize	動	企画する
outfit	名	服装
over and over	副	何度も、繰り返し
overseas	形	海外の

P

paint	動	塗る
pantry	名	食糧庫
park	動	駐車する
participate in	成句	〜に参加する
passenger	名	乗客
pastime	名	気晴らし、娯楽
patient	名	患者
payroll	名	給料支払い名簿
performance	名	演技、公演
permit	動	許可する

photocopier	名	コピー機
photographer	名	カメラマン
physical	形	身体の
physical condition	名	体調
physician	名	内科医、医者
physics	名	物理学
picturesque	形	絵のように美しい
pity	名	残念な気持ち
place an order	句	注文する、発注する
planet	名	惑星
plastic	名	プラスチック、ビニール
plumber	名	配管工
policy	名	方針
population	名	人口
position	名	職、仕事の口
postpone	動	延期する
prefecture	名	県、府
prepare	動	準備する
presentation	名	プレゼン
president	名	社長、院長、学長、大統領
previous	形	前の、以前の
print	動	印刷する
priority	名	優先事項
procure	動	調達する
product	名	製品、商品
professor	名	教授
profit	名	利益
progress	名	進歩、前進
promote	動	昇進させる
promotion campaign	名	販売促進キャンペーン
properly	副	適切に
public transportation	名	公共交通機関
publish	動	出版する
punctuality	名	時間厳守
purchase	動	購入する
put off	動	延期する

Q			rub	動	こする	
qualification	名	資格	rush	動	駆け込む	
quality control	名	品質管理	résumé	名	履歴書	

R			**S**			
rack	名	棚	sales department	名	販売営業部	
R&D department	名	研究開発部門	sales report	名	販売報告書	
rare	形	まれな	satisfactory	形	満足のいく	
rate	名	率	save	動	保存する	
recall	動	回収する、リコールする	scream	動	叫ぶ、絶叫する	
receive	動	受け取る	seat	動	着席させる	
receptionist	名	受付係	secretary	名	秘書	
recommend	動	推薦する、勧める	seminar	名	研究会、セミナー	
recover	動	回復する	senior editor	名	編集主任	
recruit	名	新入社員	serve	動	給仕する、出す	
redesign	動	デザインを改める	settle	動	解決する	
refuel	動	燃料を補給する	share	動	共同使用する	
refund	名	返金	ship	動	発送する	
regarding	前	～に関して	shop	動	買い物をする	
register for	成句	～に登録する	shopper	名	買い物客	
regular fee	名	通常料金	shrine	名	神社	
regularly	副	定期的に	sightseeing spot	名	観光地	
regulation	名	規制、規則	sign	動	署名する	
rehabilitation	名	リハビリ	sign up for	成句	～に申し込む、～に登録する	
reject	動	拒否する	sink	名	流し台	
release	動	発売する	slap	動	平手打ちする、ビンタする	
	名	発売	soundly	副	ぐっすりと	
renew	動	更新する	spam	名	迷惑メール	
renovation	名	改装	specialize in	成句	～を専門とする	
repair	動	修理する	splendid	形	素晴らしい	
reply	動	返答する、返事する	spectator	名	観客	
require	動	～を必要とする	spreadsheet	名	表計算	
rescue	動	救助する	stamp	名	切手	
resign	動	辞任する	staple	動	ホッチキスで止める	
retirement	名	定年退職	starve	動	飢える	
review	動	見直す	state	名	州	
right now	副	今すぐに	steal	動	盗む	
robbery	名	強盗				

study abroad	句	留学する
subject	名	被験者
submit	動	提出する
subordinate	名	部下
subscribe to	成句	〜を定期購読する
suite	名	スイートルーム
supervisor	名	監督者、上司
supplement	名	栄養補助食品、サプリ
supply	動	供給する
	名	備品
surround	動	取り囲む
suspicion	名	疑い、容疑

T

take	動	（薬を）飲む
take a rest	句	休憩する
take a shower	句	シャワーを浴びる
take off	成句	脱ぐ
take part in	成句	〜に参加する
take place	成句	開催される
tax	名	税金
temporarily	副	一時的に
temporary staff	名	パート社員、派遣社員
term	名	学期
term paper	名	学期末レポート
terrible	形	ひどい
thin	形	薄い
toothache	名	歯痛
town council	名	町議会
training officer	名	研修担当者、指導員
transfer	動	送金する、転勤させる
transportation	名	輸送手段、移動手段

trash can	名	ゴミ箱
turn off	成句	うんざりさせる
turn out	成句	〜であることがわかる

U

uncertain	形	不確かな
unfortunately	副	不運にも
unprofitable	形	利益のない
unreasonable	形	無理な、理不尽な
upcoming	形	次回の

V

various	形	様々な
vase	名	花瓶
vehicle	名	車両、乗り物
vending machine	名	自動販売機
vice president	名	副社長、副会長
voice-activated	形	音声作動式の
vote	動	投票する

W

wake	動	起こす、目を覚まさせる
walk a dog	句	犬の散歩をする
warehouse	名	倉庫
weekly	形	毎週の、週に1回の
weight	名	体重、重さ
withdraw	動	引き出す
work out	成句	運動する
work overtime	句	残業する
workshop	名	研修会

Workout 1　代名詞・名詞の単複　　解答用紙

No._____　氏名_____

1

人称代名詞	1人称	1.	2.	3.	4.
		5.	6.	7.	8.
	2人称	9.	10.	11.	12.
	3人称	13.	14.	15.	16.
		17.	18.	19.	20.
		21.	22.	23.	
		24.	25.	26.	27.
指示代名詞		28.	29.	30.	31.

2

1.	2.	3.	4.	5.
6.	7.	8.	9.	10.

3

1.	2.	3.	4.	5.
6.	7.	8.	9.	10.

4

1.	2.	3.	4.	5.
6.	7.	8.	9.	10.

5

1.
2.
3.
4.
5.
6.
7.
8.
9.
10.

6

1.
2.
3.
4.
5.
6.
7.
8.
9.
10.

Workout 2　Be 動詞　　解答用紙

No._____　**氏名**_____

1

	1.	2.	3.	4.	5.	6.
現在						
過去	7.	8.	9.	10.	11.	12.

2

1.	2.	3.	4.	5.
6.	7.	8.	9.	10.

3

1.
①
②
③
④
⑤
⑥

2.
①
②
③
④
⑤
⑥
⑦
⑧

3.

①

②

③

④

⑤

⑥

⑦

⑧

4.

①

②

③

④

⑤

⑥

⑦

4

1. .

2. ?

3. ?

4. The ?

5. Yesterday Jim .

Workout 3　進行形　　解答用紙①

No._____　氏名_____

1

1.	2.	3.	4.	5.
6.	7.	8.	9.	10.

2

1.	2.	3.	4.	5.

3

1.
①
②
③
④
⑤
⑥
⑦
⑧
⑨

2.
①
②
③
④
⑤
⑥

⑦

⑧

⑨

3.
①

②

③

④

⑤

⑥

⑦

⑧

⑨

4.
①

②

③

④

⑤

⑥

⑦

⑧

⑨

Workout 3　進行形　　解答用紙②

No._____　氏名_____

4

1.
2.
3.
4.
5.

5

1. We _____ then.
2. _____ ?
3. _____ ?
4. _____ ?
5. _____ ?

Workout 4　命令文　　解答用紙①

No._____　氏名_____

1

1.	2.	3.	4.	5.

2

1.
①
②
③
④
⑤
⑥
⑦
⑧
⑨

2.
①
②
③
④
⑤
⑥
⑦
⑧
⑨

3.
①
②
③
④
⑤
⑥
⑦
⑧
⑨

4.
①
②
③
④
⑤
⑥
⑦
⑧
⑨

Workout 4　命令文　　解答用紙②

No._____　**氏名**_____

3

1.
2.
3.
4.
5.

4

1.   .
2.   ?
3.   .
4.   .
5.   .

Workout 5　一般動詞［現在・過去］　　解答用紙①

No._____　**氏名**_____

1

1.		6.	
2.		7.	
3.		8.	
4.		9.	
5.		10.	

11.		16.	
12.		17.	
13.		18.	
14.		19.	
15.		20.	

2

1.	2.	3.	4.	5.
6.	7.	8.	9.	10.

3

1.
①
②
③
④
⑤
⑥

⑦

⑧

2.
①

②

③

④

⑤

⑥

⑦

⑧

3.
①

②

③

④

⑤

⑥

⑦

⑧

Workout 5　一般動詞［現在・過去］　　解答用紙②

No._____　氏名_____

4.
①
②
③
④
⑤
⑥
⑦
⑧

4

1.
2.
3.
4.
5.

Workout 6　受動態　解答用紙

No._____　氏名_____

1

1.		6.	
2.		7.	
3.		8.	
4.		9.	
5.		10.	

11.		16.	
12.		17.	
13.		18.	
14.		19.	
15.		20.	

2

1.	2.	3.	4.	5.
6.	7.	8.		9.
10.		11.	12.	13.
14.	15.	16.	17.	18.
19.	20.	21.	22.	

3

1.	2.	3.	4.	5.
6.	7.	8.	9.	10.

1. *The Old Man and the Sea* was _____ _____ Ernest Hemingway.
2. The law of universal gravitation was _____ _____ Newton in 1665.
3. Many buildings _____ _____ _____ from here.
4. I am very _____ _____ your new product.
5. Was he _____ _____ Moscow?

5

1.
2.
3.
4.
5.

Workout 7　現在完了　解答用紙

No.＿＿＿＿＿＿＿＿＿＿　氏名＿＿＿＿＿＿＿＿＿＿＿＿

1

1.		6.	
2.		7.	
3.		8.	
4.		9.	
5.		10.	

2

結果	1.　出発	2.　出発	
完了	3.　見つけ	4.　到着	
経験	5.　宿泊	6.　登　　　　　ない	
	7.　観た		
継続	8.　知	9.　住	

3

1. My husband _____ home.
2. I _____ whom to vote for yet.
3. Have you _____ Christmas cards yet?
4. Mr. MacLaine _____ his glasses.
5. He _____ the application several times.

4

1.
The soccer game _____ _____ _____.

2.
The subway _____ _____ at the station _____.

3.
_____ you _____ a contract _____?

4.
How _____ _____ have you been to China on business?
— _____ _____.

5.
Six months _____ _____ _____ they got married.

5

1.
① I have _____ in Fukuoka _____ 15 years.

② I have _____ in Fukuoka _____ 2011.

③ _____ _____ _____ you _____ in Fukuoka?

④ I _____ _____ in Fukuoka _____.

⑤ I _____ _____ _____ in Fukuoka.

⑥ _____ you _____ _____ in Fukuoka?

2.
① Cindy _____ _____ John _____ eight years.

② Cindy _____ _____ John _____ last August.

③ Cindy _____ _____ _____ John.

④ Cindy _____ _____ _____ John.

⑤ Cindy _____ _____ John _____.

⑥ _____ Cindy _____ John _____?

Workout 8　助動詞　　解答用紙

No._____　氏名_____

1

助動詞	1.	2.	3.	4.
	5.	6.	7.	8.

意味	9. 尽くす　　　　　だ	10.	11. 話すことが
	12.	13. 来　　　　　よ	14. 借り　　　ですか
	15. いる	16. 勉強	17. いる
	18. 喫煙	19. 脱が　　　ですよ	20. 謝る　　　　だ
	21. いる　　　　　だ		

2

1. I _____ be back in a few hours.
2. All the people _____ know the news tomorrow.
3. We_____ get a refund on our taxes.
4. You had lunch a little while ago, so you _____ be hungry now.
5. You _____ order anything you like.
6. This _____ be the last chance.
7. _____ _____ reply to you by e-mail?
   — No, she _____ _____ _____.
8. Malcolm _____ remember Hurricane Katrina.
9. I _____ _____ _____ _____ make him change his mind.
10. Applicants _____ _____ _____ _____ speak fluent Chinese.

3

1.
2.
3.
4.
5.

4

1. ?
2. You .
3. They .
4. An accountant .
5. We Future Media Inc.

Workout 9　不定詞　解答用紙

No._____　氏名_____

1

1. 医者に	2. 寺社を	3. チラシを
4.　　　　　　　こと	5. システムを	6. 採用通知を
7. 備品を	8. 電話に	
9. 販促キャンペーンを		10. この機器の
11. 一人でその本棚を	12. その講習会には	
13. 私を寮に		

2

1. Didn't Jackson decide _____ _____ jobs?

2. Barry has many colleagues _____ _____ him.

3. You can have a chance _____ _____ the splendid scene.

4. Ms. Schneider visited the head office _____ _____ her payroll.

5. It is important _____ _____ a report before handing it in.

3

1.	2.	3.	4.	5.

4

1.
① I　　　　　　　　　　　　　　　　　　　　　　　　　　　　　　　　　　　　　.

② I　　　　　　　　　　　　　　　　　　　　　　　　　　　　　　　　　　　　　.

③ My　　　　　　　　　　　　　　　　　　　　　　　　　　　　　　　　　　　　.

④ I　　　　　　　　　　　　　　　　　　　　　　　　　　　　　　　　　　　　　.

2.

① He _____ .

② He _____ .

③ He _____ .

④ He _____ .

3.

① They have _____ .

② They _____ .

③ I _____ .

④ It _____ .

5

1. It began _____ _____ when my daughter got home.

2. I had much homework _____ _____ yesterday.

3. We didn't have _____ _____ _____ .

4. Angela wants to learn _____ _____ _____ .

5. The cupboard was too heavy _____ him _____ move.

6

1. Kimmy _____ .

2. I _____ right now.

3. If _____ , _____ .

4. I _____ .

5. _____ ?

Workout 10　動名詞　　解答用紙

No._____　　氏名_____

1

1. 毎日りんごを1個	2. 月例報告書を
3. DVD を	4. 顧客からの意見を
5. 人前で	6. リーダー育成セミナーに
7. デザートを	8. あなたに

2

1. _____ well is essential for your mental and physical health.
2. His favorite pastime is _____ motorcycles.
3. Daniel Panther put off _____ his latest novel *The Woods*.
4. I was able to lose weight _____ _____ regularly.
5. Ms. Scott is in charge of _____ transportation for when we arrive in New York.

3

1.	2.	3.	4.	5.
6.	7.	8.	9.	10.

4

1. His job is _____ a bus.
2. _____ how to use Excel is important for you.
3. We really enjoyed _____ many attractions in the amusement park.
4. Betty was drunk and doesn't _____ slapping Greg in the face.
5. Don't be afraid of _____ mistakes when you speak English.
6. My father is _____ at cooking.

7.	Jeremy is fond _____ _____ rare stamps.
8.	How _____ _____ this over lunch?
9.	I accidentally closed a file _____ _____ it.
10.	Make sure to lock the door _____ _____ the office.

5

1.
2.
3.
4.
5.
6.

6

1. .
2. I .
3. Our team .
4. Netful .
5. .

Workout 11　分詞　　解答用紙

No._____　氏名_____

1

1.	2.
3.	4. 出てきた
5. ままだった	6. にした
7. のを目撃した	8. のを聞いた
9. 男の子	10. マックスの隣に　女性
11. カップ	12. 先月　商品
13.	14. 観客

2

1.	2.	3.	4.	5.

3

1.	2.	3.	4.	5.
6.	7.	8.	9.	10.

4

1. The zoo keeper sat _____ by rabbits.
2. The supervisor kept _____ the new regulations.
3. The manager noticed something _____ in the kitchen.
4. I saw the cat on top of the tree _____ by a firefighter.
5. The management training seminar yesterday was _____.

5

1. I am   .
2. You can   lot.
3.   at Angela Station.
4.   on October 1.
5. Children   .

Workout 12　接続詞　　解答用紙

No.＿＿＿＿＿＿＿＿＿　氏名＿＿＿＿＿＿＿＿＿＿

1

1.	2.
3.	4.
5.	6.
7.	8.
9.	10.
11.	12.
13. ＿＿＿＿＿＿　＿＿＿＿＿＿	14.
15.	16.
17.	18.
19.	20.
21.	22.
23.	24.

2

1.	2.	3.	4.	5.
6.	7.	8.	9.	10.

3

1.	＿＿＿＿＿＿＿＿＿ Alex called the dental clinic, the office was closed.
2.	Most commuters read the news on their smartphone ＿＿＿＿＿＿＿＿＿ they are riding the train.
3.	I have been a huge fan of the photographer ＿＿＿＿＿＿＿＿＿ I bought his photo book.
4.	Mr. Sanders was transferred to the sales department ＿＿＿＿＿＿＿＿＿ they are short of staff.

5.	_____ _____ the issue has been settled, you don't have to worry about it.
6.	_____ I was supposed to go to Hokkaido by plane, the flight was canceled due to mechanical trouble.
7.	Would you use my laptop _____ a new one is delivered?
8.	Look at the board in the staff room, _____ you won't get important messages.
9.	_____ _____ _____ I know, Thomas didn't apply for the position of assistant.
10.	He wanted to drink _____ coffee _____ cola.

4

1.	2.	3.	4.	5.
6.	7.	8.	9.	10.

5

1.	2.	3.	4.
5.	6.	7.	8.
9.	10.		

Workout 13 前置詞   解答用紙

No._____   氏名_____

1

1.	2.	3.	4.
5.	6.	7.	8.
9.	10.	11.	12.
13.	14.	15.	16.

2

1.	2.	3.	4.	5.
6.	7.	8.	9.	10.

3

1.	2.	3.	4.	5.
6.	7.	8.	9.	10.

4

1.	2.	3.	4.	5.
6.	7.	8.	9.	10.

5

1. The vice president got on the elevator _____ the secretary.
2. Rachel has been learning calligraphy _____ 10 years.
3. The flight _____ Tokyo _____ Amsterdam takes about 12 hours.
4. Sharon went _____ the bank to withdraw some money.
5. I had a terrible headache _____ the movie.

6. The stylish café near the station is open all _____ the year.
7. My neighbor has two rabbits _____ brown fur.
8. I was seated _____ Mark.
9. We made travel plans for our holidays _____ coffee.
10. Conrad threw the envelope into the trash can _____ opening it.

Workout 14　関係詞　解答用紙

No._____　氏名_____

1

1.	2.	3.	4.	5.

2

1.	2.	3.	4.	5.

3

1.	2.	3.	4.	5.

4

1.
2.
3.
4.
5.

5

1. Don't you remember the professor _____ taught us European Culture at university?
2. The young woman _____ we decided to employ has many qualifications.
3. The closing ceremony took place in the conference hall _____ Mr. Leonard had delivered a keynote speech about ecosystems before.
4. _____ he _____ and _____ at the party turned off their guests.
5. My guests from Canada visited the temple _____ garden was very picturesque.
6. The large screen display _____ they installed in the domed stadium is very light and thin.

7. The municipal bus is the only public transportation _____ takes visitors to Penguin Aquarium.

8. Our team hasn't decided the day _____ we will start the promotion campaign.

9. I'm afraid to ask him the reason _____ he failed the job interview.

10. Mr. Baker is the most competent attorney _____ I have ever met.

Workout 15　重要構文　解答用紙

No._____　氏名_____

1

1. _____ is generally believed _____ she was innocent.
2. _____ seems _____ Mr. White misunderstood what I said.
3. _____ will take at least three weeks for my grandmother _____ recover from the illness.
4. _____ is dangerous _____ swim in this river in spring.
5. _____ is only natural _____ they reject such an unreasonable request.
6. _____ doesn't really matter what university you graduated from.
7. His subordinates _____ the president "Emperor Nero" behind his back.
8. Senior citizens _____ the electric massager difficult to use.
9. He forgot that he _____ his dog chained up to a tree in the park.
10. The mere sight of the brochure of a horror film _____ my son scared.

2

1.	2.	3.	4.	5.
6.	7.	8.	9.	10.

3

1.
2.
3.
4.
5.

1. _____ is likely _____ my father's operation will be a success.
2. _____ was difficult for Jeremy _____ _____ the spreadsheet software.
3. _____ is necessary _____ _____ your clients in person.
4. The terrible toothache _____ Deborah awake all night.
5. We _____ Ms. Wilkinson city councilwoman in 2017.

5

1. It   contract.
2. It   .
3. Would   September?
4.   .
5.   where she was born.

Grammar Workouts!
大学生のための文法ドリル

2019年1月20日 初版第1刷発行
2024年2月20日 初版第4刷発行

著者 安丸雅子
渡邉晶子

発行者 福岡正人
発行所 株式会社 金星堂
（〒101-0051）東京都千代田区神田神保町 3-21
Tel.(03) 3263-3828（営業部）
(03) 3263-3997（編集部）
Fax(03) 3263-0716
https://www.kinsei-do.co.jp

編集担当／松本明子　　　　　　　　　　Printed in Japan
印刷所・製本所／三美印刷株式会社
本書の無断複製・複写は著作権法上での例外を除き禁じられています。本書を代行業者等の第三者に依頼してスキャンやデジタル化することは、たとえ個人や家庭内での利用であっても認められておりません。
落丁・乱丁本はお取り替えいたします。

ISBN978-4-7647-4085-3　　C1082